EDUCATIONAL SERIES

Investment Club Operations *Handbook*

Written by Jon Katz
for the National Association of Investors Corporation

Published by National Association of Investors Corporation (NAIC)
Madison Heights, Michigan
Copyright © 2004

© 2004 by National Association of Investors Corporation
All Rights Reserved

First published in the United States of America by
National Association of Investors Corporation (NAIC)
711 West 13 Mile Road, Madison Heights, Michigan 48071
1-877-275-6242 • www.better-investing.org

Manufactured in the United States of America
ISBN # 0-9678130-7-7

Katz, John 1949–

   NAIC Investment Club Operations Handbook / written
by Jon Katz for the National Association of Investors
Corporation.
   p. cm. — (NAIC Better Investing Educational Series)
   Includes bibliographical references and index.
   ISBN 0-9678130-7-7

   1. Investment Clubs. 2. Investments. 3. Finance, Personal.
I. National Association of Investors Corporation.
II. Title.

HG4532.K38 2003   332.63'22'068
                   QBI03-200322

NAIC Registered Trademark Rights

BETTER INVESTING®
BI®
BETTER INVESTING BITS®
BETTER INVESTING NATIONAL CONVENTION®
BOND FUND CHECK LIST®
BOND FUND TREND REPORT®
BOND FUND COMPARISON GUIDE©
COMPUFAIR®
COMPUFEST®
COMPUFORUM®
CREATING AMERICA'S NEXT 50 MILLION INVESTORS ®
INVESTING FOR LIFE®
INVESTFEST®
INVESTORS CONGRESS®
INVESTORS EXPO®
INVESTORS FAIR®
INVESTORS TOOLKIT®

NAIC®
NAIC FIXED INCOME MUTUAL FUND COMPARISON GUIDE©
NAIC'S YOUNG MONEY MATTERS®
NAIC...Where Main Street Meets Wall Street® (& stylized sign post)
NATIONAL ASSOCIATION OF INVESTORS CORPORATION®
OFFICIAL NAIC MUTUAL FUND HANDBOOK©
OWN YOUR SHARE OF AMERICA®
PERT®
PORTFOLIO MANAGEMENT GUIDE®
SSG PLUS®
STOCK CHECKLIST®
STOCK COMPARISON GUIDE®
STOCK FUND CHECK LIST®
STOCK FUND TREND REPORT®
STOCK FUND COMPARISON GUIDE ©
STOCK SELECTION GUIDE ®
STOCK SELECTION GUIDE AND REPORT ®

NAIC Better Investing Book Series

The Better Investing book series is designed to provide information and tools to help individuals and investment clubs become successful long-term investors. By using the series, investors will follow a self-learning pathway, gaining knowledge and building experience to make informed investment decisions. The series provides information and resources for beginners, intermediate and experienced investors.
For more information contact NAIC: 1-877-275-6242, or visit the NAIC Web Site: www.better-investing.org

Acknowledgements

NAIC Investment Club Operations *Handbook*

Author/Writer:	Jon Katz
Executive Editor:	Jeffery Fox, CFA Director, Educational Development, NAIC
Editorial Consultant:	Barrie Borich
Index Consultant:	Kathleen Paparchontis
Educational Content Consultants:	Kenneth Janke, Chairman, NAIC Richard Holthaus, President & CEO, NAIC Thomas O'Hara, Chairman Emeritus, NAIC Robert O'Hara, Vice President, Business Development, NAIC Jonathan Strong, Director, Corporate Development, NAIC Karen Bartley, Manager, Member Services, NAIC Dr. Jean Reehling, Content reviewer Evonne Hurst, Content reviewer Linda Blay, Content reviewer Melody Baldwin, Content reviewer Marvin Kohn, Content reviewer Chris Ditri, CD Advisor, NAIC
Creative Direction & Design:	Michael Bell Carol Wyatt
Design Consultants:	Ellada Azariah, Graphic Designer, NAIC Pamela Pohl, Graphic Designer, NAIC Mary Treppa, Online Editor, NAIC Mary Clyma, NAIC
Production Coordinator:	Renee Ross, Childers Printing & Graphics, Inc.
Printing/ Production:	Childers Printing & Graphics, Inc. Printwell Acquisitions, Inc.

Table of Contents

Information on the CD-ROM

(Permission is granted to copy files for personal use)

A Successful Investment Club—Slides

Glossary of Financial Terms

Investment Club Start-up List

Invitation Letter Sample

General Partnership Agreement Sample

Comments on Partnership Agreement

Club Operating Procedures Sample

General Meeting Agenda Sample

Club Meeting Minutes Sample

Clubs in Cyberspace

Keeping Clubs Together

NAIC Basic Investing Course—Slides

NAIC SSG and Report Course—Slides

Foreword

Investment clubs have existed in the United States for over a century. The oldest known club began operation in 1882 and is still in existence. The Boston based club is The Hamilton Trust and was originally known as the Hamilton Association. That investment club was and continues to be a serious endeavor, but many of the other earlier clubs were built around a combination of like social interests with little attempt to establish uniform principles for investing.

The birth of the modern investment club movement began in Detroit in 1940. Frederick C. Russell had a desire to buy a small business, wishing to accumulate capital. In speaking with George A. Nicholson, Jr., Fred was introduced to the possibility of forming an investment club. George wanted the Mutual Investment Club of Detroit to be a serious undertaking and gave the members three principles to follow: (1) Invest regularly, (2) reinvest all earnings and (3) buy growth companies. Each principle was adopted for safety, but the three in combination produced aggressive results over the years.

With the progress of the Mutual Investment Club of Detroit, the possibility of forming the National Association of Investment Clubs (NAIC) was first discussed in 1949. On October 20, 1951 NAIC was founded at the Rackham Building with four clubs as charter members. One of the major objectives of the association was to make it an educational organization. The emphasis on education continues today. The association formed a Board of Trustees of which Thomas E. O'Hara, a member of the Mutual Investment Club of Detroit, became chairman. It was through the tireless efforts of Nicholson and O'Hara that NAIC has thrived through the years.

Having traveled extensively, George found great interest in investment club work abroad. NAIC took the lead in establishing the World Federation of Investment Clubs on July 8, 1960 in London. The founding associations were NAIC, United States; NAIC, Great Britain; the National Bureau voor Beleggings Studieclubs, the Netherlands; and the Federation of New Zealand Investment Clubs. That organization has grown to include associations from Australia, Austria, Belgium, Canada, Czech Republic, Denmark, Estonia, Finland, France, Germany, Hong Kong, Japan, Norway and Sweden.

The experience that individuals can derive from belonging to an investment club can help in many ways. Not only can a small, regular investment in a club eventually grow to a significant amount, but the principles can benefit members in their personal investment program. It is not unusual for a new investment club member to have no experience in the stock market. After gaining knowledge by putting a relatively small amount of money at risk, confidence grows and a member begins to build a personal portfolio. Investment clubs are a wonderful way to introduce people to the benefits of equity investing. It is our hope that your experience will be a good one and only the first step you take to financial independence.

Kenneth S. Janke

CHAIRMAN
NATIONAL ASSOCIATION OF INVESTORS CORPORATION

Introduction

Imagine an America with almost twice as many people as there are today. Over four hundred million folks fighting for every inch of space, every scrap of food, every ounce of security for themselves and their heirs.

We'll be facing such a muddle during the middle of the century. Are you ready to start preparing for it now?

Before you answer, let's turn the premise around. Go back in time to 1940 and tell the 132,000,000 people living in the United States that within two generations the population will double, that a dollar for a gallon of gas will be a bargain, that Social Security and pensions will not maintain the lifestyle of the country's senior citizens.

How many Americans back then would have started to put away a portion of their paychecks for an outrageous eventuality that today is our reality? A country weary of depression and worried about war was clearly focused on the present and compelled to let the future take care of itself.

There were some, however, who saw the need and seized the opportunity. They were not visionaries, nor were they the rich who sought to get richer. They were regular folk with new families and old cars. But they believed in free enterprise and felt that it was not beyond the average worker to invest wisely in it. Better yet, by putting their heads as well as their dollars together, they could reap the benefits of this strength in numbers and make them last beyond their own lifetimes.

Thus was the formation of the Mutual Investment Club of Detroit.

It would be the stuff of Hollywood fiction to say "Little did they know," because clearly the tremendous growth in their membership and assets—indeed, the reason you're reading this book today—was part of their goal from the get-go. It's in the words they put down in 1951 when they created the Trust that formed

show a profit during that same period or even longer.

Stick with it. Trust in a proven long-term investment philosophy and you'll follow in the footsteps of thousands who have financed their children's education, traveled the world and avoided money worries in retirement.

And had a great time doing so.

the foundation of what is now the National Association of Investors Corporation:

"The purpose of this Trust is to aid in the preserving and strengthening of democratic capitalism by educating people in...investment principles..."

Note that they didn't say anything about making money. It's in there implicitly, of course; let's not kid ourselves about why we're here. However, developing the means to the end is precisely the purpose of NAIC. The combined power of education and time-tested investment principles are themes you'll encounter

regularly during your reading and during your meetings.

That and something else: the power of patience. As you'll learn in the very first chapter, many investment clubs dissolve within the first eighteen months. The primary reason is that too many members bring a get-rich-quick mentality to the table, along with the fact that new clubs typically don't

A Word to Our Readers

Forming and operating an investment club is easier than assembling your kid's bike. Why, then, should the instructions be as hard or harder? They shouldn't.

In putting this handbook together, the general reader has always been uppermost in mind. The approach is therefore light and moderately low-tech. Using an easy-to-read Q&A format, we address your questions and your concerns, your objectives and your objections.

You'll also hear from many of our members who've learned and profited from the journey on which you're about to embark. We're confident that their words will be helpful and inspiring.

Throughout the book, you'll be encouraged to take advantage of NAIC's extraordinary inventory of tools and support. They're as close as your keyboard or phone, and ready to work for you even now. The Chapter Notes will also point the way to additional sources of knowledge.

You'll also find a tremendous amount of information, advice and even fun on the enclosed CD-ROM. A subject list is provided in the Table of Contents.

Welcome to the world of investing the NAIC way.

NOTE: All information contained in this book is designed and provided for educational value and is believed to be accurate as of the date of publication. It is not meant, nor should it be considered to be, specific investment, tax or legal advice. Readers should consult professionals in these areas to discuss their specific situations.

Investing the NAIC Way

What Is NAIC?

Before we begin, there's one thing I don't get.

What's that?

Why is a book about investing clubs being written by the New Italian American Citizens— the NIAC?

Congratulations. You've just proved one of our more important investing tips. "Pay attention to details."

Well anyway, who are you guys: a company, a club, a broker, what?

The National Association of Investors Corporation—that's NAIC—is a nonprofit, tax-exempt volunteer organization whose membership consists of investment clubs and individual investors.

How many?

At press time, over 210,000 individual and investment-club members, with over 20,000 clubs registered nationwide. We like to think of NAIC as the voice of the individual investor.

Why?

The individual investor drives the American economy. According to the New York Stock Exchange (NYSE) 2000 Shareowner Study, nearly 75 million Americans are

shareholders, and that number continues to grow. The individual investor has learned that intelligent investing in stocks can build wealth.

NAIC recognizes the value of providing investor education to everyone—young and old, men and women, minorities and other groups. NAIC provides educational support at the local, state and national levels. We work with governmental groups, corporations and other organizations to advance

investor education and maintain a level playing field.

What do you mean?

At one time, individual investors were the major force in the market, directly owning more than 80% of the stock of U.S. corporations. Today, individuals directly own less than 50% of all corporate equities. But that's still almost half, making it critical that these shares be bought—and held and sold—as a result of sound investment information, education and support. It is

On October 20, 1951, The National Association of Investment Clubs was founded at the Rackham Building, Detroit, with the Mutual Investment Club of Detroit and two other Michigan clubs as charter members.[1]

Chairman Emeritus Thomas E. O'Hara has served the organization since its inception; Chairman Kenneth Janke, Sr. has been with the NAIC since 1960. (Writings by O'Hara and Janke, referenced in this manual, are informed by the chairmen's decades of experience with NAIC.)

NAIC President and CEO Richard A. Holthaus assumed his current duties in early 2002. He is well known to many NAIC volunteers, having served on the organization's board of trustees for 15 years. Holthaus was previously a senior vice president and senior partner of St. Louis based Fleishman-Hillard Inc., where he was co-leader of the company's financial communications group.

NAIC's Proven Investing Philosophy

Today's most successful investment clubs—with assets of hundreds of thousands of dollars, a million dollars or more—started out with only a few dollars.

C'mon. A few dollars?

That's right; a $20, $30, $50 monthly investment from each member can grow to stunning

to that end that NAIC has provided investment education to over five million Americans since 1951.

That long?

Even longer, really. The Mutual Investment Club of Detroit, which you'll learn more about in Chapter Two, was founded in 1940. As a result of its success, the creation of a national association was pursued with vigor.

NAIC's MISSION
To provide individuals and investment clubs with a program of sound investment information, education and support that helps create successful lifetime investors.

NAIC IS NOT...
• *A commissioned investment advisor*
• *A stock broker or consultant*
• *Short-term oriented*
• *Company stock specific*

NAIC DOES NOT...
• *Recommend investments*
• *Teach stock market timing techniques*

amounts—and has. We know because over the years, our member clubs have achieved results that would make most professional money managers envious.

One word: how?

The NAIC approach to investing is a long-term strategic buy-and-hold method that's not as popular with hotshot "advisors" and "planners" as other pie-in-the-sky approaches.

It is founded on a fundamental analysis of a company (i.e. focusing on company sales/revenues, earnings, P/E ratio and how management is driving growth), rather than just a technical analysis of stock performance (i.e. focusing on stock price moves, market momentum or short-term indicators). It revolves around NAIC's four basic investment principles. Here they are:

NAIC's Four Basic Investment Principles

1. *Invest on a regular basis over a long period of time.*

2. *Reinvest all earnings, dividends and profits.*

3. *Buy growth stocks and equity mutual funds.*

4. *Diversify your portfolio to reduce risk.*

And that's it?

Pretty much. There's more to it, of course, but you'll find that you don't need a seat on the stock exchange to follow these principles and benefit from them. The same philosophy that helped so many before you to achieve consistently superior results can work for you and your club. All it takes is the will, the discipline and the patience to apply them.

PRINCIPLE ONE:
Invest Regularly Over a Long Period of Time

You'll enjoy two benefits from this simple principle. The first one is the discipline of dedicating a set amount of

money toward building your portfolio. The second benefit is even more tangible: dollar cost averaging.

Now that I've heard of, but nobody I ask is able to explain it to me.

Let's give it a try. Dollar cost averaging means investing roughly equal amounts of money regularly in the same stock or fund. That constant amount invested will buy more shares when the stock price is down, fewer shares when the price is up. Over time, you'll buy most of your shares at a cost lower than the average price.

FIGURE 1-01: DOLLAR COST AVERAGING

Month	Amount Invested	Stock Price	Shares Bought
1	$ 25.00	$ 15.00	1.666
2	$ 25.00	$ 15.50	1.612
3	$ 25.00	$ 16.00	1.562
4	$ 25.00	$ 16.50	1.515
5	$ 25.00	$ 17.00	1.470
6	$ 25.00	$ 17.50	1.428
7	$ 25.00	$ 18.00	1.388
8	$ 25.00	$ 18.50	1.351
9	$ 25.00	$ 19.00	1.315
10	$ 25.00	$ 19.50	1.282
11	$ 25.00	$ 20.00	1.250
12	$ 25.00	$ 20.50	1.219
Total	$ 300.00	$ 213.00	17.058
Average	$ 25.00	$ 17.75	17.590

ONE-YEAR SUMMARY

Total Investment:	$ 300.00
Total Shares Purchased:	17.058
Average Cost per Share:	$ 17.59
Portfolio Value:	$ 349.69

Let's say you invest $25 a month in Stock "A" over the course of one year. Here's how you'll do (See Figure 1-01):

Note that the average cost per share—the price you actually paid—was $17.59, lower than the $17.75 average price of those same shares. In fact, since the value of those 17.058 shares at the year-end price of $20.50 is $349.69, and you paid only $300 for them, you made a 16.56% profit.

And *that's* dollar cost averaging.

Sounds doable to me.

In fact, investment clubs are the perfect setting for taking advantage of dollar cost

averaging, says Ben Baldwin, an NAIC member and president of a Northbrook, Illinois-based financial counseling firm. "Just the fact that investment clubs usually invest each and every month into a variety of different stocks means you're taking advantage of dollar cost averaging as well as diversification," he said.[2] (Diversification is the subject of Principle Four).

In essence, clubs dollar cost average in two ways. First, by investing regularly each month. Second, by purchasing more shares of the specific stocks that are in the buy zone that month.

But doesn't regular investing also mean more broker commissions?

Good point, and all the more reason for a solid commitment to the methods of selection taught by NAIC. As for stock and fund transactions, Chapter Seven will get into the use of Direct Purchase and Dividend Reinvestment Plans (DRPs) to bypass brokerage fees.

And now, before we move on to Principle Two, bear in mind this early warning signal:

A significant number of investment clubs go out of business within the first eighteen months because of conflict between those who believe in long-term investing and those who advocate speculative trading.

For some interesting final thoughts on Principle One from NAIC Chairman Ken Janke, please see the accompanying sidebar: "Invest Regularly" Means "Invest Regularly"

PRINCIPLE TWO:
Reinvest All Earnings, Dividends and Profits

This principle gets to the heart of the matter: saving vs. investing.

There's a difference?

Take a look. The term saving usually refers to putting money aside for the future. In a savings bank account, your money may earn a bit of interest, but the real reason you save is to have money on hand when you need it. Everybody should have some money in an interest-bearing account; the instant liquidity it offers may come in handy.

Investing is something else again. When you invest, you are taking intelligent steps to make your money grow over time. Investing in stocks and mutual funds involves risk, and you have to know something about the companies and/or funds you are investing in. But if you do your homework and invest wisely over an extended period, investing is a proven and powerful way of increasing your wealth.

Part of that power is what we call "The Magic of Compounding."

"INVEST REGULARLY" MEANS INVEST REGULARLY
BY KENNETH S. JANKE, SR.

Following the events of September 11, 2001 the Dow Jones Industrial Average plunged almost 1,400 points in one week. Many investors sold their holdings, some never to return. The decline in stock prices was actually a continuation of what we had been experiencing during the past year, but was accelerated by the terrorist attacks.

At times of trauma and uncertainty we tend to forget the importance of (NAIC's) first principle for building wealth over the long term—regular investing.

While many Wall Streeters have been saying, "Hold on," I think the real words of wisdom go one step further. They are, "Continue to buy." Whether you belong to an investment club, invest as an individual or both, regular investing should be a part of your master plan if you want to build wealth over the years in a safe and sure way.

Proof of the benefit of regular investing can come from looking at a chart of any of the popular common stock benchmark indexes. Two things become obvious immediately. One is that the long-term trend has been up. As population and demand continue to grow, fueling increased sales and earnings, stock prices of well-managed companies will do the same. The second observation is that there are many ups and downs in market prices on the way to the new peaks.

During 1973-74 those who accumulated shares of stock while the market continued to decline eventually were richly rewarded. The same was true after the market drops in 1987 and 1989. It takes courage to continue to invest when the near-term outlook appears to be one of gloom and doom.

History has shown that no matter how prolonged a bear market might be, in the long run regular investing pays off. Remember to follow the first NAIC investing principle. It may sound simple, but it works.[3]

Doesn't money compound in my savings account?

We don't think that a 1- or 2-percent annual interest is exactly the "power" you and your club are looking for. By reinvesting earnings, dividends and profits, the money you make is put back into your investments. Think of your portfolio as a snowball rolling down a hill, picking up more snow and growing larger and larger with its own momentum.

Figure 1-02 shows what $10,000 invested at various annual rates of return may yield. You and your club may not have that amount immediately available to commit; the figures, however, do suggest starting to invest now, at whatever amount is comfortable.

PRINCIPLE THREE:
Buy Growth Stocks and Equity Mutual Funds

Growth companies are usually defined as companies that are growing faster than the rate of growth in the overall U.S. economy. Quality growth companies should have established continuous growth records for sales and earnings for at least five years and preferably longer.

FIGURE 1-02: COMPOUNDING

$10,000 INVESTED AT COMPOUND RATES

Rate of Return	10 Years	20 Years	30 Years
3%	$ 13,440	$ 18,060	$ 24,270
5%	$ 16,290	$ 26,530	$ 43,220
8%	$ 21,590	$ 46,610	$ 100,630
10%	$ 25,940	$ 67,280	$ 175,490
12%	$ 31,058	$ 96,462	$ 299,597
15%	$ 40,456	$ 163,665	$ 662,118

Is there a specific reason for that?

It's been shown that continuous growth reflects strong management. You're interested in such quality growth companies because you will be seeking consistent above average annual growth in net earnings over the next five years.

The Goal?

NAIC suggests that you set a goal of doubling your investments every five years. This is accomplished by obtaining a 15% (actually, 14.87%) total return on your investment, consisting of price appreciation plus dividend income, compounded annually. Remember the Rule of 72.

72?

The Rule of 72 says that, if an asset grows x% a year, its value will double in 72 ÷ x years. Divide 72 by the annual rate of return to see how long your investment will take to double.

Thus, if an asset is growing at 10% a year, 72 ÷ 10 = 7.2 years.

The Rule of 72 is also used to calculate what rate of return

is required to double your money in x number of years.

To double your investment in five years, you'll have to realize a 14.87% rate of return compounded annually ($72 \div 5 = 14.87\%$).

And is that possible today?

You're not thinking about today—you're thinking about tomorrow, a tomorrow years down the road. And over time, yes, it's possible, even probable. Many NAIC members and member clubs have been consistently successful at setting and achieving their goals, including beating the S&P 500 Index, a commonly used benchmark to measure stock performance.

How do they do it so well?

Mainly by following these Four Principles, the third of which advises to invest in growth stocks and equity growth mutual funds. NAIC forms and software tools help them find profitable investment choices. These tools will be introduced later.

PRINCIPLE FOUR:
Diversify Your Portfolio to Reduce Risk

This is the "Don't put all your eggs in one basket" principle. But it goes further than not dumping a disproportionate amount of your investment dollars into a high-flying tech stock or a company that was profiled in the latest issue of a financial magazine (excluding NAIC's *Better Investing,* of course). You need to diversify your portfolio both horizontally and vertically.

Well if you wanted to confuse me, congratulations.

Sorry, we got a little ahead. The horizontal-vertical diversification concept actually comes to us from Billy Williams of Atlanta. Billy's been investing the NAIC way since the 1960s, currently serves as chairman of the NAIC Atlanta Chapter and is himself a member of three different investment clubs.

Billy recommends to new clubs that they select one industry to study each month. Then, using the NAIC Stock Selection Guide (SSG), choose the best company in that industry to add to its portfolio. This is, he calls it, horizontal diversification.

Going vertical, he stresses that "it's important to keep in mind that diversification also means choosing different-sized companies [because they're] affected differently by the economy and the stock market's ups and downs in the same way companies in various industries are affected differently. This should give your portfolio a broad base of diversification."[4]

NAIC's tools will be invaluable in guiding your vertical as well as horizontal searches for quality companies.

The Benefits of Investing for a Lifetime

We won't spend a lot of time or space convincing you of the benefits you'll derive from becoming an individual or club investor. You're reading this to help you increase those benefits. Nevertheless, let's review five great reasons to stay on the path you've now chosen.

The rewards of investing can last a lifetime.

Financial success grows out of the assets you build up over time. Investing brings the deeper and more lasting rewards of security and economic power that come from accumulation of wealth.

Time is on your side.

Stock prices go up and down. But over the long haul, stock prices have always gone up, and patient investors will profit from that trend. In addition, reinvesting earnings will grow those profits at an ever-increasing rate.

Investing can help you beat inflation.

Prices have a tendency to rise over time as well. This is called inflation. If your wages rise at the same rate, you're keeping pace with inflation. If, however, your interest earning checking or savings account remains at its present rate, you are losing money—or more accurately, you are losing purchasing power. The dollar you get back is no longer worth the dollar you put in. Intelligent investing produces a return on your money greater than the rate of inflation. You are taking the teeth out of inflation's bite.

Investing is a way of owning a piece of corporate America.

The money you invest helps companies continue to do business. If the companies make a profit, you can claim your share of it. You own a piece of the pie and you are helping to sustain America's growth.

Investing is fun.

You sometimes hear the radio and TV commentators refer to the stock market as gambling. Is investing a form of gambling? In certain sectors of investing (i.e. penny stocks, options, futures), the answer is yes, with one overriding difference. On the Las Vegas strip or the Atlantic City boardwalk, the advantage is always with the house. On Wall Street, the advantage is with the informed investor. Sometimes you'll play a hunch and roll the dice in both places. But the investors who win consistently base their choices on research and reliable information. That is where NAIC can help put the odds in your favor!

Investing in Stocks & Mutual Funds

OK, if you can put the odds in my favor, start by telling me why my club and I should invest in stocks and mutual funds when there are so many choices out there.

In the beginning, there is always the fear and concern of possibly losing money, coupled with the wonder and excitement of building a significant profit. As you become familiar with stock selection and ownership, many of these mysteries will disappear and you will become as confident in picking stocks and funds as you are buying meats and vegetables at the grocery store.

Because you can start investing with small amounts, previous experience is not required. Your knowledge will grow as the amount of money you regularly invest does the same.

As a general rule, investment clubs do **NOT** invest in mutual funds. Why? Because an investment club is **YOUR** own fund, managed by you. To put mutual funds in it will be a duplication of effort and fees. The exception to this rule is when a club puts a very specific sector type mutual fund (i.e. international fund) in the portfolio.

Is it true that investing in common stocks has been the safest way to invest?

"Safe" is a term that is difficult to prove or disprove. Research by Robert G. Ibbotson, a nationally recognized authority on market returns, shows that over the past 70 years, the ownership of common stock has been—by far—the most profitable of all major forms of capital investment.[5] Over time, stock ownership has provided the greatest investment opportunity to the largest number of Americans. Owning stock in a well-run, growth-oriented American business can bring tremendous benefits to you and your loved ones.

And what about mutual funds?

The answer to that question is worthy of an entire book in itself. In fact, we've written one: *NAIC Mutual Fund Handbook*. We invite you to consult it for anything you need to know on the subject.

Briefly, mutual funds are pools of money from various sources, from individuals to global corporations. Professionals who are paid to devote full time to making investment decisions manage this money.

These funds can invest their pooled money in a variety of ways, such as a portfolio of stocks (equities), bonds or money market instruments. You, the shareholder, own a

proportionate part of the fund, much the way you'd be a part owner of an individual company in which you purchase stock. If an equity fund invests in 50 stocks, you own a part of those 50 stocks.[6]

What are the advantages of mutual funds?

Mutual funds offer a broad variety of advantages that make it a vehicle of choice for millions of investors, novice to pro.

Diversification. By its very nature, a mutual fund will maintain a list of holdings that's larger than what you would likely have as an individual or a club. This may offer you protection against fluctuations in one area of the market or from a negative earnings report from one specific stock. Most importantly, you get this protection at a fraction of the sum you'd pay were you to buy a large number of individual securities.

Professional Management. Your money will be handled by a person (or persons) who can devote more time to your investment than you can. However, their levels of expertise and track records vary widely. By using NAIC resources and tools, you will be able to select fund managers who successfully invest in growth companies for the long term.

Convenience. Fund shares may be purchased and sold easily, by phone or computer. Automatic transfers from your personal or club bank account make regular investing a snap. Likewise for automatic reinvesting of dividends and capital gains distributions.

Selection. There are well over 10,000 mutual funds from which to choose. Some invest in thousands of individual stocks, others in only a handful representing a single "sector," such as energy or communications.

Liquidity. Shares can be redeemed on any trading day at their "net asset value," which is announced at the end of trading.

Investor Information. In response to pressure from the Securities and Exchange Commission (SEC), the fund prospectus and shareholder reports have become streamlined and demystified.

Protection. The SEC maintains stringent regulations on mutual fund transactions and on the funds themselves.[7]

There must be some disadvantages to mutual funds.

Indeed there are, but with proper research and diligence, you can turn each one into an advantage.

No Guarantees. Unlike bank deposits, your investment is not protected by any federal agency. Risks are inherent with mutual funds as much as with individual stocks.

Management Ability. While professional management is noted above as an advantage, we must repeat here that these managers are only human. Their stock picking ability can vary widely. They can also be limited by the investing philosophy of the fund itself. Use NAIC tools and software to research track records.

Diversification Flop. Investing in a large group of stocks insulates the investor somewhat from taking a huge loss, but the strategy also limits the upside you might enjoy with a smaller concentrated portfolio of individual stocks. Diversification is a risk reduction feature because it spreads risk. It does not increase the earnings potential of a portfolio.

Fees. Without careful selection, you may find that transaction costs for mutual funds exceed the cost of direct investment in stocks. Be aware of front-end sales charges (loads), back-end or exit fees and ongoing operating expenses that compromise returns.

Capital Gains. When a fund manager sells a stock in the fund, it triggers a taxable event for all fund shareholders with taxable accounts. You'll find enormous differences among funds, and it is their tax-adjusted returns that are most meaningful. These figures will make it clear which funds should be in tax-deferred accounts and which funds work well outside of tax-deferred accounts.[8]

Summary

The National Association of Investors Corporation is a non-profit, tax-exempt educational organization whose membership consists of investment clubs and individual investors. We like to think of NAIC as the educator of the individual investor.

On October 20, 1951, The National Association of Investment Clubs was founded at the Rackham Building, Detroit, with the Mutual Investment Club of Detroit and two other Michigan clubs as charter members.

NAIC's Mission is to provide individuals and investment clubs with a program of sound investment information, education and support that helps create successful lifetime investors.

The NAIC approach to investing is a long-term strategic buy-and-hold method that is based on four basic investing principles: invest on a regular basis over a long period of time; reinvest all earnings, dividends and profits; buy growth stocks and equity mutual funds; and diversify your portfolio to reduce risk.

The evidence to date is that NAIC principles are likely to give the investor consistent, long term investment results. NAIC established the Top 100 Stocks Index, dating back to 1986, based on the 100 most widely held stocks by NAIC members. That index has regularly outperformed the Dow Jones Industrials and the S&P 500.

Five great reasons to be an individual or club investor: the rewards of investing can last a lifetime; time is on your side; investing can help you beat inflation; investing is a way of owning a piece of corporate America; investing is fun.

Over the past 70 years, the ownership of common stock has been—by far—the most profitable of all major forms of capital investment.

Mutual funds offer a broad variety of advantages that make it a vehicle of choice for millions of investors, novice to pro. There are also disadvantages that can be overcome with proper research and diligence. Mutual funds are normally not purchased for investment clubs.

Chapter Notes

[1] Thomas E. O'Hara and Kenneth S. Janke, Sr., *Starting and Running a Profitable Investment Club* (New York: Times Books, 1998) vi.

[2] Amy T. Rauch-Bank, "Beginner's Corner," *Better Investing* April 1998: 72.

[3] Kenneth S. Janke, Sr., "'Invest Regularly' Means Invest Regularly," *Better Investing* December 2001: 12.

[4] Amy T. Rauch-Neilson, "Weeding and Feeding Your Portfolio," *Better Investing* May 2001: 68.

[5] Ibbotson Associates, Chicago, Illinois.

[6] Jon Katz, *Investing For Life: The NAIC Mutual Fund Handbook* (Madison Hts., Michigan: 2000) 17.

[7] Katz 23-25.

[8] Katz 26-28.

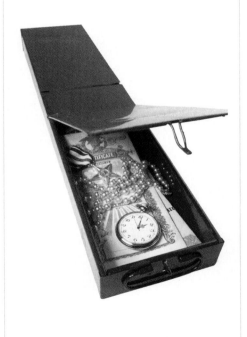

Introduction to Investment Clubs

A Background on Investment Clubs

The Mutual Investment Club of Detroit and the Founding of NAIC

How an Investment Club Can Help You

Success of Investment Clubs over Time

Essential Elements: Check for Success!

Summary

Now that we've cruised through the obligatory "who we are and what we do" portion, let's get to what you're doing here. You want to form an investment club or perhaps you already have.

Chapter 2 through Chapter 10 will guide you through the process, untangle the legalese and stock-speak, and help you achieve the three purposes of all our clubs: education, profit and fun.

For organizational purposes, we'll assume that you're just forming your club and that you'll be following along as we take you through it step by step. For those of you using this handbook as a tool to give your club a "tune-up," you may certainly skip portions of this chapter.

"No pain, no gain" may be fine for a fitness video, but these are not the words of encouragement you and your fellow members will hear from us. Deciding where to invest your retirement fund or your kid's college dollars shouldn't be painful. And it isn't. It is work; make no mistake. But it's work that will pay off, very literally. And yes, you'll also learn stuff and have fun in the process.

So on with the show. Let's begin at the beginning.

A Background on Investment Clubs

What exactly is an investment club?

An investment club is a group of people—generally 10 to 20—who come together to learn from each other to build and manage a growing portfolio of stocks and other securities.

Club members can include friends, family, co-workers, neighbors, church and community group members, and others you know.

I thought investment clubs only included family members.

Well, to quote Tina Turner, "What's love got to do with it?" Seriously, clubs composed entirely of family members are a surprisingly small percentage of the over 23,000 NAIC-affiliated clubs currently out there. We'll get into the task of finding members for your club in the next chapter,

Whether you're a raw rookie or a seasoned veteran, investment clubs are an effective way to become a more successful investor.

I understand that investment clubs began in Detroit around 1940, right?

Those are NAIC's roots, but actually, investment clubs go back to the late 19th century.

The oldest known investment club still in operation today is The Hamilton Trust, an investment club created in Boston in January 1882.

The next oldest known club began operations in Texas in 1898. A. L. Brooks, a member of that club, later joined several NAIC-affiliated clubs. Most of the early clubs were formed as social organizations with combined investing as one activity. There was little, if any, attempt to establish uniform principles for the guidance and education of members.[1]

The Mutual Investment Club of Detroit and the Founding of NAIC

So what happened in 1940?

NAIC co-founder George A. Nicholson (1908–1996) was the impetus for the founding of the Mutual Investment Club of Detroit in February of that year.

"How can we argue for free enterprise if we do not own it broadly?" he would later write

but in a pinch, you can even contact other clubs in your area by attending and networking at local NAIC chapter events. In addition, many of our members belong to multiple clubs.

I'm concerned about people joining for the wrong reason. Specifically, our timetables for accumulating wealth may differ widely.

You really hit an important nail right on the head. And be assured, we will be delving deeply into making sure you're all on the same page before going too far with organizing your club. For now, let's state clearly that investment clubs are not a get-rich-quick scheme.

In the first year or two, many clubs may show only small gains or even some losses. As club members become more knowledgeable, their expectations and results become greater and more consistent with the realities of investing.

Meanwhile, for the new investor, clubs provide a great way to begin to understand investing in a systematic learning environment. For experienced investors, clubs are valuable to sharpen investing skills, gain new ideas from others, uncover new opportunities from meetings and keep up-to-date on economic trends.

in the 1953 Harvard Business School Bulletin. "Perhaps there would be no communist problem in the world if most families owned $5,000 or $10,000 of common stocks." His passion was to help make that happen.[2]

Nicholson, a Harvard-educated security analyst, believed there were three necessary ingredients to building widespread support for and participation in the free enterprise system: principles to go by, ways to learn and goals to achieve. He saw investment clubs as a means to providing all three.

At the close of 1939, one of the young charges at his Detroit brokerage house was a go-getter named Fred Russell. Under Nicholson's "silent" guidance, a meeting was arranged at Russell's house for any of his interested young friends and any of their interested young friends. One of the "friend-of-a-friend" invitees was Tom O'Hara.

A twenty-four-year-old junior assistant with the Ernst and Ernst accounting firm in Downtown Detroit, O'Hara was earning eighteen dollars a week but dreaming of much more. In fact, he had been following the financial section of the newspaper since his days at Southwestern High School, scribbling out imaginary investments in his notebook.

On February 1, 1940, a group of twelve men met, anteed up their first month's dues of ten dollars each, and signed the letter of agreement establishing The Club. That's what they called it—"The Club."

They had no idea what a positive influence their actions would have on millions of people. As for themselves, they would all become millionaires. Most of them several times over.[3]

And then, in 1951...

Not so fast. "The Club," soon after renamed the Mutual Investment Club of Detroit, was George Nicholson's grand experiment. If what his young protégées were attempting gained a foothold, Nicholson saw it as the model for a nationwide movement. An association of many such clubs, he figured, made up of everyday people owning shares in leading corporations, would make for a stronger America. But before that could happen, individual investors needed to be educated.

Nicholson patiently designed and then directed the slow but steady development of the Mutual Investment Club and its members.[4]

"Seeing the progress of the club and noting the way the club members advanced their family finances and businesses, the subject of a national association was first discussed seriously in 1949," recalled Nicholson.[5]

In fact, Tom O'Hara had been campaigning for just such expansion since the end of World War II. "We need more clubs," Nicholson told him, "more examples that prove this concept really works."[6]

Nicholson had been instrumental in forming two other Detroit-area clubs. On August 28, 1951, representatives of the three clubs met to sign an historic Trust Agreement.

"The purpose of this Trust is to aid in the preserving and strengthening of democratic capitalism by educating people in the investment principles that have and are now being employed by members of the Mutual Investment Club of Detroit, Michigan, the Pontiac Investment Club of Pontiac, Michigan and the One Hundred Ten Club of Ann Arbor, Michigan."[7]

The new Trustees, led by Tom O'Hara, set an organizing convention for Saturday, October 20, 1951 at Detroit's Rackham Building. Membership in the new organization was priced at one dollar.

Sixty-five people registered and 12 clubs became charter members at the founding meeting. George Nicholson gave the keynote address.[8] His stirring words would ring true for generations to come.

> "The significance of our action today might not be known for many years. Quite possibly, it will turn out to be much ado about nothing. But any time a movement grows out of the grass roots of America, as this one has done, and secures the active participation of so many men and women of all ages and circumstances, it has, to say the least, the potential of wielding a vast influence... To be sure, it is no atom bomb, but it has, perhaps, a greater explosive power."
>
> *George A Nicholson, Jr.*
> *Keynote Address*
> *Founding of the National Association of Investors Clubs*
> *October 20, 1951*

Those gentlemen certainly were visionaries.

And their vision was certainly shared. Within two years more than 100 clubs and 1500 individuals became members of the Association. By the end of the first decade, clubs anxious to bring NAIC investing principles to life in their region established nine regional chapters, then called councils. The modern day investment club movement was on its way.[9]

How an Investment Club Can Help You

So what happened to the Mutual Investment Club of Detroit?

Why not ask them? The club still exists. And with a portfolio currently worth over $7 million—not including the over $4 million previously distributed to its members—it's a serious understatement to say they're still going strong.

But even so, why form or join a club when I can do the same thing myself?

Ah, there's the $64,000 question—or maybe the $10 million question. Perhaps Tom O'Hara could've done it himself, too. He didn't think so. The point is, he saw three reasons to hook up with other like-minded men over sixty

years ago, and these reasons remain the primary goals of NAIC club members today.

Those are great reasons to form or join a club. But they still don't tell me the ADVANTAGES of investing as a member of a group versus as an individual.

OK, how about these:

ADVANTAGE: Buying power.

Have you tried telling a broker you've got $25, $30 or $50 to put into something solid? Commissions from even deep discount Internet brokers will eat you up. It's a bit like one of the advantages of a mutual fund: the ability to own dozens or even hundreds of stocks without the commissions associated with buying them separately. Combine your $30 with $30 from a dozen friends, and you've got enough money to get some attention and save some serious money on commissions, while at the same time establishing your club as a regular customer.

THE REASONS TO START AN INVESTMENT CLUB (BASED ON NAIC SURVEYS)

1. EDUCATION. A vast majority of club members are new to investing. Together, they learn while they earn. What's more, they learn from each other. An organization has weight that an individual does not to obtain the services of guest speakers, arrange field trips to corporations and gather specialized research information, with the ultimate benefit of making more knowledgeable investment decisions.

2. PROFIT. Being "in it for the money" to the exclusion of all else probably won't make you a happy club camper. It's not the only reason to join. But let's get real—it's certainly one of the top three!

3. SOCIAL INTERACTION. Getting together monthly with family and friends—old and new— makes for a pleasant couple of hours away from the daily grind. The most enduring clubs are those that successfully mix pleasure with business. Throughout this book, we'll illustrate how they do it.

ADVANTAGE: *Division of labor.*

Now really, are you prepared to spend the kind of time it takes to do the kind of research all by yourself that a club can take on as a group? With eleven other members, you may have to make only one stock presentation a year. And you get to be the beneficiary of all their work.

ADVANTAGE: *Spreading risks and Sharing rewards.*

Along with group buying power comes safety in numbers. Like having lots of friends with flashlights to help find a lost object in the dark, you're not alone out there searching through the mysterious shadows of stock selection.

ADVANTAGE: *Forced discipline.*

There isn't a parent alive who hasn't said to a complaining child, "Hey kid, homework never stops." The group structure of an investment club and the operations requirements you all agree to provide a positive incentive to pull your own weight. You'll also find

ADVANTAGE: *Affordability.*

Can you find $30 or so every month? Granted, many of us may have to think about that some months. Instead, think about this: can you save $30 every month from somewhere else? One less dinner out? Wait for the movie to come out on tape or disc? Repair the heel on those shoes instead of...well, you get the idea.

that kicking in that monthly contribution will soon seem as habitual as paying the phone bill, and a lot less painful.

I can't argue with any of those advantages. But are there DISADVANTAGES to an investment club?

To be perfectly honest, any disadvantages are likely to be the reverse view of one of the advantages named above. In other words, there are admittedly people who plainly are not "cut out" for the club life, which is no negative reflection on them. For example, any commitment of time—even spread out amongst 12, 15 or 20 members—may be perceived as too much of a commitment.

An investment club that follows NAIC principles will make stock selections only after extraordinary diligence. Such decision-making may be too slow for some, the buy-and-hold strategy too long-lasting for some.

One must recognize that an investment club is different than most social groups, in which 80 percent of the work is done by 20 percent of the people. In an investment club, 100 percent of the work is achieved by the equal efforts of 100 percent of the members.

That's why they work.

Success of Investment Clubs over Time

NAIC's oldest club is also one of its great success stories. What follows in Figure 2-02 is the financial history of the Mutual Investment Club of Detroit. Shown are the members' total accumulated deposits and reinvested earnings, withdrawals and liquidating value.

During the war years of the 1940s, the club participants did not put new money into the club because many of them were in

the service. Withdrawals were made at various times for down payments on homes, education expenses for children and even to start new businesses.

Note that in the early years, initial deposits were small, but consistent contributions grew into a large investment portfolio. Although your club may not amass a multi-million dollar portfolio, you can see that the financial opportunities are impressive, indeed. Your club can obtain positive

performance rates by following and using the NAIC method.

Original Mutual Investment Club member and NAIC Chairman Emeritus Tom O'Hara is, understandably, often asked for advice and commentary by financial authors. He has offered these words. "Start as early as you can, even if you're retired, because you may have twenty years ahead of you. Don't worry about saving only small amounts [and] don't get discouraged."[10]

| | | | Earnings from Sales of Securities and | | Withdrawals Value Feb. 28 | |
FIGURE 2-02: A CASE STUDY—The History of the Mutual Investment Club of Detroit						
Year Ended Dec. 31	Total Accumulated Deposits by Members	Earnings from Dividends	Reinvested Earnings	Accumulated Total Deposit	Following Year	Liquidating
1941	800	—	—	800	—	812
1945	5,080	—	—	5,080	—	9,844
1950	8,741	1,100	167	15,041	3,000	20,690
1960	40,885	3,701	11,012	109,326	—	151,515
1970	84,083	11,696	3,498	271,333	2,955	394,434
1980	133,640	19,003	67,171	649,035	25,750	915,726
1990	275,130	59,865	55,591	1,606,878	105,321	1,833,368
1995	425,960	59,581	10,593	2,896,800	445,285	3,002,181
2000	607,845	70,374	386,759	3,883,430	653,090	7,061,518
TOTAL	607,845	1,197,828	2,077,757	3,883,430	4,049,486	7,061,518

NAIC solicited its 50 oldest clubs to share their individual stories for inclusion in its monthly *Better Investing* magazine during 2002. Here are two:

TYCOONS OF 1023 GRAND, KANSAS CITY, MISSOURI
BY LLOYD BRIGGS

The Tycoons of 1023 Grand was founded in December 1954 by H. Roe Bartle, who at that time was the Chief Scout executive for the Kansas City Area Council of the Boy Scouts of America. He believed the people who worked for the Boy Scouts should learn about investing. The Scout headquarters was located at 1023 Grand in Kansas City, so the club became the Tycoons of 1023 Grand.

All of the original charter members are deceased, but they established the basic investment philosophy that stocks should be carefully evaluated and investments made for the long term.

In the beginning club meetings were held in the Scout office. But over the years as the membership changed, the wives were invited and the meetings moved to the members' homes. Over time the meetings have become more of a social event, with the members and their wives meeting for dinner at a restaurant close to the home of the meeting's host.

Our broker frequently attends our meetings and provides current information on the stocks in our portfolio which, along with the Investor Advisory Service, can be used by members to report on their stocks.

Over the years the club has paid substantial amounts to estates of deceased members and members who have resigned from the club. In addition, several past and present members have received payments for partial withdrawals. I personally do not recall a withdrawal on which there was a loss on the member's investment.

Our investment club has been a source of fun and fellowship as we share our common interest with one another while providing an opportunity to invest for the future.[11]

FIGURE 2-03: TYCOONS INVESTMENT CLUB

DEL BRAZO ASSOCIATES INVESTMENT CLUB, LOS ALAMOS, NEW MEXICO
BY RICHARD MARTIN

When Del Brazo Associates Investment Club was founded in 1955 no one without appropriate government credentials could even visit because it was the site of the National Laboratory, where the first atomic bombs were developed and built. Los Alamos has changed dramatically since then, But while the membership roster is different, of course member interests haven't really changed since the club's birth.

The club still is keenly interested in understanding the investment process, in learning about various stock offerings and in enjoying the unique camaraderie that grows from our shared interests. When we look back through club records, we notice that the early members seemed more willing to take a flyer on penny stocks and local stocks than we are today.

In earlier times Del Brazo meetings were followed by poker games that went on through the night; one suspects that on some nights, the buy and sell discussions were rushed to get to the card game. Today, stock purchase decisions usually are preceded by lengthy discussion and analysis, including the preparation of an NAIC Stock Selection Guide.

The current portfolio of 21 stocks is worth $550,000. For about 12 years beginning in 1988, it seemed like we could make no wrong investment choices. The portfolio value rose steadily from around $90,000 to almost $790,000.

The club considers and acts on buy and sell proposals only at our regular meetings, so decisions on a particular stock are sparse. A system like this naturally leads to a buy-and-hold stance. This strategy has served the club well. Most members are in the club for investment education as well as for investment opportunity.

"Del Brazo" derives from a Spanish idiom meaning "arm-in-arm." The name reflects the Spanish heritage of New Mexico and describes how our members approach the investment challenge. We have leveraged the sharing of knowledge and techniques to improve the return on our individual portfolios as well as that of the club. We have a good time doing that.[12]

FIGURE 2-04: DEL BRAZO ASSOCIATES CLUB

Essential Elements: Check for Success!

So have you noticed a pattern yet?

It seems clear that the successful clubs are the ones that subscribe to and follow NAIC's four principles.

It would be pretty obvious—and self-serving—to base this whole book on just those principles, although their importance cannot be overestimated. Starting with the next chapter, we'll begin to follow a formula that will take your new club through its first two years, and beyond.

Right now, let's quickly look at some of the elements that no successful club can afford to ignore. We will bring out each in greater detail as we progress through the process of making your club successful in its own right.

Before we do that: what's the last thing that aircraft pilots do before taking off?

They go through their pre-flight checklist.

Exactly. So before your club takes off, we've come up with a checklist of items that no successful club can ignore. You can check back on your checklist as you continue your reading, and you might even prepare it as a handout for your first organizational meeting. Observing these start-up and ongoing tips will help to ensure that your club is properly organized and prepared to use NAIC's time-tested methods for successful investing.

So check these out:

How the Top Clubs Survive and Thrive

Select Club Members Carefully. Choose from family members, co-workers, neighbors or others you know from organizations such as church, fraternal groups or social clubs. Include members who will offer a diversity of backgrounds, occupations and knowledge. This will help generate new ideas and provide interesting discussions and debates at your monthly club meetings. (See "Demand Active Membership" below).

Agree on a Common Investment Philosophy. Include people in your club who will follow a similar and compatible investing philosophy and goal. A long-term investing approach that focuses on selecting leadership growth companies has been proven to be successful, as opposed to a short-term, market timing approach.

Schedule Your First Regular Club Meeting ASAP. Within the first two start-up meetings, it is important to set a regular meeting date and location to increase attendance. Your club should also set a goal and agree upon the date that first stock presentations and investments will be made. The length of time can vary between clubs, but is typically three-four months.

Complete the Club Enrollment and Start-Up Information ASAP. Adopt your club partnership agreement and operating procedures; elect officers; register your club with the IRS and local/county/state offices; join NAIC.

Start a Regular Educational Program. It is essential to start and follow a regular educational program at each club meeting, teaching members how to analyze and review companies for potential investment. During the year, each member will be asked to make presentations on new stocks or those currently in your portfolio. Run the club like a business; be punctual, organized, orderly and efficient. Set clear expectations regarding the time members will spend preparing for meetings.

Keep It Simple. Don't let members get discouraged by having to use a calculator. Tracking your investments will involve numbers—no getting around it. Choose a good treasurer who will learn and use the proper investment club accounting techniques. You'll all get the hang of it soon enough.

Delegate! Don't let a few members carry the weight. There is a lot of research work, information gathering and discussion planning that must be accomplished regularly. Discover hidden or unused talents of club members and delegate appropriate tasks to each of them.

NOTE: In NAIC's experience, there are, inevitably, some clubs whose work does fall on only a few members. Most of these clubs succeed because these active members really enjoy their jobs. At the same time, you as an individual will not further your investment skill if you don't participate. Force yourself to prepare

studies of corporations, and you will find the sense of accomplishment is great! Clubs should consider it a priority to involve everyone by scheduling stock study presentations in rotation throughout the year.

Fun! Fun! Fun! A slow or bear stock market may cause unrest and even discordance amongst the members. Other causes include a "sameness" in the people and the meeting dynamics. Keep the meeting part of the meeting business-like and formal, then break out and have some laughs. We'll offer many more suggestions to put a little spice into stock picking in Chapter 5.

Conduct Meetings Conveniently and Regularly. Pick times and places that make it workable for everyone. Note that some clubs bypass December altogether. Whatever your schedule, stick to it! A little rain or someone's last-minute tickets to a play aren't cause for cancellation. They only show that your club may not be disciplined enough to be an investment club.

Demand Active Membership. Members coming to meetings to eat cookies and get stock tips in return for the grace of their presence aren't the kind you want coming around, even if they're family. You want members who will participate and contribute to the learning experience. And if you won't act, the SEC will. They've got something called "passive membership" on the books, and they don't look kindly on it. To find out more, go to www.sec.gov.

Remember—It's a Business. This is not a put-down of sewing circles or poker nights. Just don't forget that your club is formally and legally registered with numerous governmental agencies, not the least of which is the IRS. Conduct the club's business as if it was your own family business. In so many ways, it is. You might also want to consider bonding, which is discussed further in this book.

Have Patience, Persistence, Confidence...and More Patience. It took those Mutual Investment Club guys some 60 years to get where they are today. Many younger investors have never been through a genuine bear market. Know that your approach is sound and stay with the game plan.

Remember the Rule of Five. This investment theory for intelligent portfolio management holds that of every five stocks owned over a five year period, one will be a stinker, three will perform pretty much up to expectations and one will make you a stock picking guru. When you start bragging about that last one, don't forget the first one.

Summary

An investment club is a group of people—generally 10 to 20—who come together to learn from each other to build and manage a growing portfolio of stocks and funds.

Investment clubs are not a get-rich-quick scheme. In the first year or two, many clubs may show only small gains or even some losses. As club members become more knowledgeable, their expectations and results become greater and more consistent with the realities of investing.

NAIC co-founder George A. Nicholson (1908–1996) was the impetus for the founding of the Mutual Investment Club of Detroit in February 1940. The subject of a national association was first discussed seriously in 1949.

On August 28, 1951, representatives of the Mutual Investment Club of Detroit and two other clubs met to sign an historic Trust Agreement creating the National Association of Investors Clubs.

There are three primary goals of NAIC club members today: education, profit and social interaction.

Advantages of joining an investment club include buying power, affordability, division of labor, spreading risks and sharing rewards, and forced discipline.

NAIC Chairman Emeritus Tom O'Hara advises, "Start as early as you can, even if you're retired. Don't worry about saving only small amounts and don't get discouraged."

Chapter Notes

[1] George A. Nicholson, Jr., *National Association of Investment Clubs Manual* May, 1958: 1.

[2] *Better Investing* October, 2001: 50.

[3] Mike Wendland, *From little acorns grow: Main Street Millionaires* (2000) 27.

[4] Wendland 30.

[5] Nicholson, Jr. 1.

[6] Wendland 37.

[7] Wendland 43-44.

[8] Wendland 45.

[9] *Better Investing* October, 2001: 50-51.

[10] John F. Wasik, *The Inve$tment Club Book* (New York: Warner Books 1995) 86.

[11] *Better Investing* March, 2002: 44, 56.

[12] *Better Investing* April, 2002: 28-29.

Getting Off the Ground

Ten Steps to Start Your Investment Club

Finding Members for Your Club

The Organizational Meeting

Summary

With your permission, let's continue the metaphor from the previous chapter. You've gassed up the engine, gone through that pre-flight checklist and now you're ready to take off. But you're not a helicopter; you can't just rise up and fly. You've got to roll down the runway, picking up speed the whole way, and finally, when there's enough lift under your wings, you defy gravity and gently nose up into the clear sky that waits ahead.

There are certain steps you must now take to actually start up the club in earnest. We're going to name 10 of them here, as well as the chapters in which you can find more complete details. These steps encompass everything you need to do to organize your club and, in turn, to ensure a successful experience.

So push the throttle forward and get ready to roll!

Ten Steps to Start Your Investment Club

STEP ONE:
Hold an initial meeting.

Without raising a flag to see if anyone salutes it, you can't know the viability of your brainchild. Invite people you

know who may be interested. And ask them to invite people they know. After all, where would NAIC be if that "friend of a friend" Tom O'Hara hadn't been asked to the very first such meeting in 1939? Once you've verified the interest of prospective members, it will probably take two or more of these organizational meetings to deal with the steps below, laying the groundwork for your club prior to the first official monthly meeting. More about the first exploratory

get-together follows later in this chapter.

STEP TWO:
Find members.

This critical phase is considered fully in the next section of this chapter.

STEP THREE:
Elect officers.

Ilene Meade of Zimmerman, Minnesota has started three investment clubs and served as an officer in all three. She has led numerous NAIC seminars

at a faster pace.[1] As we said, she should know.

The role of club members and officers will be explored fully in Chapter 5.

STEP FOUR:
Research the partnership agreement.

This is it, the legal document that says you're not just fooling around. At this point, take a good look at the sample NAIC General Partnership Agreement included in this book and on the accompanying CD-ROM.

In choosing between two possible forms for the club—corporation or partnership—the Mutual Investment Club of Detroit considered five questions. They're just as critical for you today:

1. **Taxes.** Under which type of organization would members pay the least in taxes from the time money was first earned until individual members received it?

2. **Personal liability.** Which type would minimize members' personal liability risk?

3. **Transfer of securities.** With which form can securities be transferred with the least need for supporting resolutions?

4. **Organizational costs.** Which type would minimize the cost of setting up the club?

5. **Maintenance costs.** From the standpoint of both time and money, which type would be more economical over the life of the club?[2]

The partnership agreement will get the full treatment in the next chapter.

STEP FIVE:
Draft operating procedures.

These are the detailed workings of the club, which should be customized to meet the needs of the members. Ilene Meade recalls that it took her Dollars and Sense Investment Club "several months of drafting before we were satisfied."[3]

You'll find everything you need to satisfy your club in the next chapter.

STEP SIX:
Register the club.

Your neighbors may wonder about all those cars in front of your house, but the U.S. government will be more than curious. You'll need the IRS Form SS-4 to properly register the club for tax purposes and get an Employer Identification Number (EIN), which you'll need, in turn, to open a bank and/or brokerage account.

on investment club operations and her teachings will be referenced often in this and future chapters.

Ilene has found it best, she says, to elect the treasurer first, followed by the president and then the rest of the slate. Their duties will be later laid out in the club's operations procedures. Once officers are installed, Ilene promises that the club's organization will move along

Next, you'll be filing a "Certificate of Conducting Business as Partners" form (also called a "Doing Business As" form). Requirements for filing this and other documents vary, so have the club secretary or treasurer contact your state secretary's office or licensing board as well as the office of your local county clerk. There may be a minimal registration fee.

Each year the club will file tax returns using IRS Form 1065. Club members must file their own club tax returns using the information from IRS Schedule K-1.

Sample forms and explanations are in Chapter 4 and Chapter 6.

STEP SEVEN:
Open bank and brokerage accounts.

Your club will need them both. But what kinds? We'll go through the options in Chapter 7.

NOTE: In some cases there is no need for a bank account, because many brokers provide the ability to write checks against a money market account in any denomination. Many clubs start with two accounts and then may eliminate the bank checking account as a duplication not needed.

STEP EIGHT:
Join NAIC.

This is the easiest step and perhaps the most important. Thousands of investment clubs have found the materials provided by NAIC to be invaluable. Indeed, brokers with years of experience with investment clubs point out that their most consistently successful clubs have been ones which make full use of NAIC's tools and services, which you'll find described more fully in all the chapters to come.

STEP NINE:
Start monthly meetings and educational programs.

Clubs that hold well-run, organized meetings

consistently enjoy superior investment results. Ask your new club president to appoint a member to prepare a report of a corporation using the NAIC Stock Check List. At the next club meeting, review the Stock Check List and then ask another member to prepare a report on the same corporation in the NAIC Stock Selection Guide. This process is for teaching purposes so that all members can begin the experience of completing and learning the use of these forms.

Monthly meetings will be discussed in Chapter 4. Your club's progression through years one and two are subjects covered in Chapter 5.

The Stock Check List and Stock Selection Guide are just two of the forms designed by NAIC to help investors analyze and evaluate stocks. Figure 3-01 offers thumbnail descriptions of NAIC's analysis forms. It will be repeated later as Figure 9-07.

FIGURE 3-01: NAIC INVESTMENT ANALYSIS FORMS

FORM	DESCRIPTION
Stock Check List (SCL)	This form helps the new investor review the basic financial information of a stock and develop an opinion of its current value. It serves as an introduction to the Stock Selection Guide.
Stock Selection Guide (SSG)	NAIC's most popular guide to stock analysis. It is designed to help you review the financial history and record of a particular stock and, using your judgment, make an informed investment decision.
Stock Selection Guide and Report (SSG&R)	NAIC's four page stock analysis guide for all investors allows you to record historical data, make future projections and interpret the results to make informed investment decisions for individual stocks.
Stock Comparison Guide (SCG)	This guide helps you make an intelligent comparison of several stocks, such as similar stocks within the same industry. It is designed to aid in the selection of the best potential investment.
Portfolio Management Guide (PMG)	Once you have purchased a stock, follow its sales and earnings record by plotting and graphing stock data over time. The PMG helps you make buy and sell decisions for each stock in your portfolio.
Portfolio Evaluation Review Technique (PERT)	With PERT and PERT Worksheets A and B, investors can follow the monthly progress of all stocks in their portfolio. Track sales, earnings, stock price and more—an essential record of all your securities and portfolio performance.
Challenge Tree Kit (CTK)	This kit and set of forms allows the experienced investor to determine whether or not to continue holding a stock or to replace it with one appearing to have greater potential.
Mutual Fund Forms	1. The Stock and Bond Mutual Fund Check Lists guide the investor through a step-by-step process that examines key elements of a fund that need to be understood prior to considering it for investment.
	2. The Stock and Bond Mutual Fund Comparison Guides help you compare different funds' performance, yield and other factors to determine a potential investment decision.
	3. The Stock and Bond Mutual Fund Trend Reports are used to log and update criteria for a particular fund purchase, and to monitor for changes.

NOTE: *NAIC provides software or tutorials that allow you to complete each of the investment analysis forms above.*

STEP TEN:
Use NAIC resources.

This is also a no-brainer. Start by attending meetings of the NAIC Regional Chapter near you. Established club members will help you get acclimated to the NAIC way. They'll also introduce you to the vast array of resources available to you as an NAIC member. You'll find a comprehensive list of NAIC-produced print, video and software in Chapter 10 and on the NAIC Web Site— www.better-investing.org. Most, if not all NAIC chapters offer classes on how to use these resources. Attending them is not only a good way to learn, but also a great opportunity to meet other investment club members with whom you can share ideas.

Finding Members for Your Club

Those steps are great. However, the first two make me nervous. How do I really go about finding other people who are serious about starting a club, who will commit to it like I will, who will bring something to the party? In other words, how do I find a dozen more of me?

Great way to put it. But what you need to realize and bear in mind is that the last thing you want is a dozen more of you.'. Certainly your fellow members should be committed to the club's success, as it impacts all

of you equally. This means, in large part, that they need to support the advocacy of NAIC's four investment principles.

You should know this: many investment clubs dissolve before their second anniversary because of investing philosophy disagreements. A club cannot exist, reminds NAIC's O'Hara and Janke, if it's divided between long-term investors who want to follow NAIC's principles and others who are determined to act as traders, moving in and out of the market. For many inexperienced first-timers, the allure of fast profits and active trading is irresistible. Successful investment clubs adhere to the more conservative point of view that wealth building is a slow process, particularly in the first few years.[4]

That said, one of the key things that will keep the club together is the membership mix. A dozen more exactly like you may avoid some debates along the way, but really, where's the fun in that?

You'll want to look for people whose individuality will be one of the main reasons to join, unless you're calling yourselves the "Clone Club."

Very funny.

Anyway, the very purpose of this book is to help your club make it through the "terrible

two's," those formative years which make or break so many clubs. Before we seek out prospective members, look at Figure 3-02 for a thumbnail sketch of NAIC members already on the rolls.

FIGURE 3-02:
NAIC MEMBERSHIP PROFILE

Average Personal Portfolio Value:
$388,000

Median Household Income:
$114,100

Average Monthly Investment:
$84

Education:
72.2% college or graduate degree

Median Age:
55.8

Individual Membership by Gender:
69% Female
31% Male

Club Membership by Gender:
54% Female
38% Mixed
8% Male

Source:
Mediamark Research, Inc. 12/03

So how do I get my group together? Who should be in the club? What kind of club should it be? Where do I find these people? When do I meet with them?

Who? What? Where? When? Slow down! Let's take it one "W" at a time.

Who Should Be in the Club?

The last chapter indicated that you should recruit club members carefully from a number of diverse sources. Family, co-workers, neighbors, church members, and social friends are all good starters. Try to avoid individuals who might "dominate" club meetings, as other members will learn more if they don't rely on one or two persons. "Furthermore," O'Hara and Janke suggest, "the collective judgment of a number of reasonable people can be much sounder than the opinion of a single source, however knowledgeable that individual might be."[5]

Whom *should* you seek out? Consider this sample of factors:

INDIVIDUAL INVESTING KNOWLEDGE.

Look for people not too far above or below your own level of experience. The assertion that club members will let the pro handle things can work both ways. If you have a fairly comfortable working knowledge of the stock market and are surrounded by pure neophytes, that makes you the pro by comparison, a position in which you plainly do not want to find yourself.

INDIVIDUAL EXPERTISE.

Each member will embody a lifetime of personal wisdom that's bound to make your whole club greater than the sum of its parts.

Take the typical housewife. No "real world" expertise, you say? Who better to evaluate the vast food and pharmaceuticals industries? Back in the 1970s, a whole lotta ladies went to the store and squeezed a whole lotta Charmin bathroom tissue. Procter and Gamble—and its investors—squeezed a whole lotta profits.

INDIVIDUAL WEALTH.

What about comparative family incomes? Should that nice lady from church whose husband has built a prosperous family business from the ground up be excluded because she's way above your own tax bracket? Absolutely not, says personal finance writer Marsha Bertrand. What if the husband's been handling all of their finances and then dies before her or divorces her? "She needs to invest her wealth to make it grow," Bertrand advises. "Not having that knowledge and suddenly becoming responsible for a huge amount of money

makes that person ripe for a con artist's wiles."[6]

INDIVIDUAL COMMITMENT.

We can't overuse the "C" word. If you're letting someone in "only" because she bakes great brownies, you're letting yourself, your fellow committed members and the club itself in for a very costly fall.

You'll find that your dependency on the others runs deep. Schedules must be kept; deadlines must be met. If a member misses her once-a-year stock presentation because her favorite aunt is in town, where does that leave the rest of you?

Author Bertrand recommends that you solicit people who display traits in their everyday lives that are essential for the success of the club. "If a person is responsive and responsible in her job," she asserts, "chances are that person will also be a responsive and responsible member of an investment club."[7]

INDIVIDUAL RESIDENCE.

The world may be smaller than it once seemed, but people still prefer to find everything they need within a few minutes travel time, workplace excluded. If your club is composed of neighbors, absenteeism will tend to be lower than in a club of business colleagues spread out over three counties.

Down the line you may be forced to make decisions concerning good members who move, but by then you will have shaken out those grumblers you were glad to see go anyway.

Note that the subjects of online clubs and family clubs with members spread out around the country are not being raised here, but will surface a bit later.

What Kind of Club Should It Be?

With that question we introduce the issues of gender, age, ethnicity and relationship.

Since 1951 NAIC has provided investment education to over five million Americans. The journey began and continued through the boom stock market of the 1950s and late 1960s. The recession of the mid-1970s caused a great deal of uncertainly, and investment club levels dwindled as it seemed the stock market would never advance again. Many investors were sidetracked during this period. The gains made in the 1980s and 1990s restored recognition of the benefits of investing and resulted in dramatic growth in the number of investment clubs.

More recently, the dot-com crash at the turn of the millennium again gave rise to a question of confidence in the market. This time, however, investors were able to recall the reasonably quick bounce-backs in the Dow Jones Industrial Average after the 1987 crash and the 1991 Gulf War, and generally stayed the course.

The loss of over 1,400 points immediately after the events of September 11, 2001 likewise did not induce widespread investor panic.

And through it all, NAIC has continued its educational mission to those five million Americans no matter who, where or how old.

GENDER.

With the passage of time, a dramatic shift in club demographics has come about. From 1955–1980, it seemed that NAIC served a predominantly male membership. Beginning in the 1980s and continuing the trend in the decade following, a large increase in the number of female members and all-female investment clubs took place.

As shown in the Membership Profile (Figure 30-2), it is estimated that 69% of NAIC members are female; further, all-female clubs account for approximately 54% of NAIC clubs in total.

Why this flip-flop in member gender? Without question, the famous Beardstown Ladies Investment Club sparked great national interest on the topic of women and investing. In addition, there's the growing population of women in the workforce, as well as an increasingly large segment of women much like the aging, newly rich church lady we met in the "Individual Wealth" subhead earlier in this chapter.

As a result, a 1999 report by the National Association of Securities Dealers (NASD) estimated that 47% of all investors in the United States were female.

Around the same time, NAIC was finding that women's clubs were performing better than both their all-male and mixed-gender counterparts (although more recently the mixed-gender clubs have turned in a solid performance record as compared to all-female and all-male clubs). The reasons—based on annual surveys, focus groups and extensive discussions—leave themselves wide open to cries of stereotyping, but here they are:

WHY WOMEN INVESTORS OFTEN DO BETTER THAN MEN

1. Women tend to conduct more thorough research before investing.

2. Women generally do not purchase or sell stocks on the latest hot tip from another source.

3. Women often look at the "whole picture" and opportunities an investment may provide, thoroughly analyzing decisions they make with their money.

4. Women tend to follow a consistent, long-term approach to investing.

5. Women stay with investments they research and purchase, riding out the ups and downs of the market and not jumping in and out of a stock quickly.

6. Women can often be more socially aware investors who ask ethical questions about the companies they investigate.

7. Women typically purchase stocks of well-known consumer companies that have proven profitable from the sale of their goods or services.

Along with these reasons for their impressive performance, NAIC has identified the top three tasks to which women must turn their attention and increase their efforts:

KEY CHALLENGES FOR WOMEN INVESTORS

1. More women in America need to start a regular investing program, making consistent contributions for future needs such as retirement programs.

2. Women need to place a greater percentage of their income in retirement investments. On average, women live longer and earn less than men; they therefore must invest larger percentages of money for the future.

3. Women need to be more confident when investing. Remember the Rule of Five: for every five stocks in your portfolio, one is likely to perform beyond expectations, three will perform as expected and one will not meet expectations. Four of the five, therefore, will provide an above-average total return over time.

AGE.

Investment clubs are better than movies. Think about it:

- You're not looking at things in the dark,

- The food's a lot better, and

- Anyone can get in.

Speaking to that last point, if NAIC's primary mission is to educate—indeed, if one of the primary goals of the clubs themselves is investment education—should there not be room, then, for the youth of America to learn and earn right alongside their parents?

The answer is a definite two thumbs up. NAIC estimates that approximately 10% of its membership is now under 30. A special NAIC Youth Membership is available for members 18 and under, which includes a subscription to NAIC's *Young Money Matters* newsletter.

But should these fresh, young investors be allowed to have their own clubs, or suffer sitting with a roomful of old folks kvetching about how they could have bought Microsoft at $2 a share?

Either way is fine, says the SEC, with certain restrictions. Minors can't purchase securities, so parents must set up a custodial account for them with a brokerage firm. This is done through the Uniform Gifts to Minors Act

(UGMA) or the Uniform Transfers to Minors Act (UTMA), depending on your state. The assets legally belong to the minor and will become theirs with no strings attached when they become 18 or 21, again depending on the state.

Joking aside, your adult friends or co-workers probably don't want your teenager in a club with them and the feeling is certain to be mutual. Better, in this case, to form a family club in which the kids can not only feel more comfortable but also can have a real voice in the family's future (see The Taffy Investment Club story below).

Forming a youth investment club, through the school or a social organization, is accomplished in much the same way as forming any other investment club. The same paperwork has to be filed and the same inner structure has to be set in place. This means that a partnership agreement must be duly drafted, which parents/guardians sign.

An adult transacts purchases and sales of securities, and a person of legal age also assumes responsibilities for the club's accounting. Other important information can be found in NAIC's youth materials.

Despite the fact that adults are ultimately the administrators of such a venture, the kids do take on many of the same "grownup" tasks and obligations, which is a benefit they'd be hard pressed to find anywhere else.

Just ask the "future millionaires," as they confidently call themselves, of The Crescents of New Orleans Investment Club.

NAIC is fully committed to youth investing programs. Dozens of chapters have selected a youth investing chairperson to help lead the local effort. NAIC has produced two youth and parent/youth educational presentations for their use to communicate money saving

and investing concepts to area students. Chapter support is offered in conjunction with NAIC/South-Western Educational Publishing's high school textbook, *Investing in Your Future.*

NAIC has also published the *Investing for Life— Youth Handbook.*

ETHNICITY.

Financial journalist and former senior editor for *Black Enterprise* magazine Carolyn M. Brown

THE CRESCENTS OF NEW ORLEANS INVESTMENT CLUB

These 12 students from Cabrini High School got the backing of parents and teachers to form their own club and put NAIC

principles into practice. They even received start-up grants from local companies and an anonymous donor.

In the first few meetings they learned how to read stock market tables and Value Line, complete the Stock Selection Guide using NAIC software, and make presentations.

Getting the club established and mastering the SSG were exercises in patience for the Crescents. It took four months before they made their first decision about which stocks to purchase (13 shares of Starbucks and 25 shares of The Gap).

The most common reaction from adult friends and relatives has been, "I wish I had learned about investing in school. You are so lucky to have this opportunity."[8]

FIGURE 3-03: CRESCENTS OF NEW ORLEANS INVESTMENT CLUB

teaches that cultural traditions for pooling money can be found in America's immigrant communities. "West Indians use susu, Africans have ekoubs, and Asians have gaes. Generally, these are family-run pools, and the money is used to set up business shops, buy homes, pay for weddings and fund education."[9]

Trouble is, they are neither legal entities nor investment vehicles. Following NAIC

principles would seem to be a much safer, stable and profitable endeavor.

Black Enterprise found that to be the case when it ran a story on investment clubs that grew out of college fraternity and sorority relationships. Among those profiled was an all-male club composed of members of Alpha Phi Alpha. NAIC's own *Better Investing* magazine also featured their story.

Carolyn M. Brown is a staunch supporter of early investing by two of America's most influential demographic segments: its minorities and its young. "If African Americans are going to begin matching their academic and economic gains of the past few decades with progress in the financial front," she writes, "it's going to require that more and more of us get down to the business of capital formation in our twenties and thirties."[11]

THE SEVEN JEWELS LEGACY INVESTMENT CLUB

The Smyrna, Ga. club has been affiliated with NAIC for five of its seven years. Its members share a vision of empowering other African Americans with investing knowledge.

"Our club avidly believes that the African-American community wields enormous economic power," says Thomas Brooks, immediate past president. "The challenge continues to be for the community to pool its resources together to make strong plays into new venues."

"We believe that the stock market, with its almost limitless potential for high growth and high earnings, is one of the frontiers that we as African Americans

can conquer," Brooks states. "With the wealth of knowledge at our fingertips, there is no reason why we should not be making successful forays into the investing panorama."

The club, by the way, got the inspiration for its name from

the seven college students, affectionately known as the "Seven Jewels," who in 1906 at Cornell University formed what was to be the oldest African-American Greek letter organization in the United States.[10]

FIGURE 3-04: SEVEN JEWELS LEGACY INVESTMENT CLUB

RELATIONSHIP.

Family clubs are a unique breed. They offer some obvious advantages; then again, they create some snags that can sneak up on you. For that reason, while family members seem like a built-in club, going that route may, in the long run, be a decision you'd like to have back.

Not so for Betty Taylor of Kansas City, Kansas. She formed the Taffy Investment Club with her family in 1987, and offers a classic case of turning obstacles into opportunities. An investment clubber since 1960, Betty is a former NAIC volunteer National Board member and the founder/past president of the Kansas City Area Chapter.

Betty Taylor does not contend that, "The family that pays together, stays together." She does, however, point out the best reason to gather your clan the way she has. "My husband and I have a portfolio that we hope our children will inherit. And we want them to have the education to be able to take care of it. We want to do everything for our loved ones."[12]

FIGURE 3-05: THE TAFFY INVESTMENT CLUB

"Now, more than ever, with so many families spread across the country or around the world, [family investment clubs] keep people connected," Betty Taylor reports. "When we started Taffy, it represented four generations of our family."

At that time, Betty's family was located in Washington State, Kansas, Georgia and Alabama. That was, of course, before e-mail. "We mailed our stock studies to each other and talked on the phone."

But being a nationwide organization of sorts gave them the early word on small local businesses with big potential. In one case, very big potential. "Our son-in-law, Joe, is a real do-it-yourselfer. He discovered Home Depot in Atlanta near where he lives [and] that became our club's first stock purchase."

Today, Taffy members are e-mailed voting sheets on

BETTY TAYLOR

which they can indicate purchasing preferences. They are also able to do stock studies by committee and forward articles on stocks to study.

Best of all, for Betty, her family club remains a family club. Children are admitted under UGMA, which was discussed above in the "Age" segment. One of the club's biggest decisions was deciding when minors could become voting members, a decision totally up

to club members and not subject to state law. "Allowing members to vote when [they are] very young and unable to make their own evaluations can be unfair," Betty says. "A family with five children would always prevail over the family with two."

Another concern with running a family business—which in almost every sense this is—involves tough love. "You tend to be more lenient," according to Betty. "We did not include a bylaw [specifying fees for late contributions] when we started the club. If I had to do it over again, I would."

Family clubs, she cautions, should also have a clause in the partnership agreement about divorce. "Thankfully, we haven't had to deal with that, [but] from what I've observed...the person who is not the blood relative leaves the club and is paid off, or the shares of the club go to their children."

Where Do I Find These People?

In a word: everywhere. A good mesh of personalities should be uppermost in your mind, but that doesn't mean you should pull people from the same secretarial pool, car pool or pool hall. The right combination may come together from delightfully diverse places. In fact, the most successful clubs are composed of individuals from a variety of backgrounds and experiences.

Consider everyone: family, neighbors, schoolmates, fellow workers, church chums, bowling buddies, everyone. And don't forget to give each of them the option of penciling in prospects of their own. We cite once again the case of Tom O'Hara who was on that secondary list back in 1939.

Authors Douglas Gerlach and Angele McQuade—each of whom has made significant contributions of time and effort to NAIC and its online initiatives—advise club organizers that the list of potential members can't be too long at this point.

"Most people you approach agree that planning for their financial future is important," say Gerlach and McQuade. "An even smaller number express an interest in actually taking a step toward accomplishing what they've planned. Even fewer...will agree to consider the possibility of starting a club with you, and only a handful will actually attend the initial planning meeting."[13]

Like laying the foundation for any structure there's bound to be a "settling in" period, and that applies to club membership as well. Aim high, say Gerlach and McQuade, to prepare for inevitable attrition as your club finds its own firm footing, a process that may take several months.

NAIC itself can also be a source of interested people. Contact the NAIC chapter near you. Attend a class on starting a new club and you'll find yourself networking in no time. You should also attend an NAIC-sponsored seminar, workshop, investor's fair or other event. Your chapter may also be one that runs a "model club" which is a full-functioning club that's open to the public. You may find notices at NAIC chapter events which post messages such as clubs looking for members.

That's right, there are some things NAIC *cannot* do, and some things *you* cannot do.

NAIC POLICY

Due to SEC regulations and for the protection and privacy of NAIC members, NAIC Headquarters and NAIC chapters cannot provide names or addresses of NAIC investment club members or individual members for the purpose of seeking an investment club to contact or join.

To learn more about investment club activities or to meet others in your region who may want to form a club, contact your NAIC Regional Chapter.

PAT McVEY-RITSICK

"My first word of advice is that clubs should be ultra-selective about the members they choose," cautions Pat McVey-Ritsick. Pat is a seasoned NAIC teacher and a member of the San Fernando Valley, California-based Women's Investment Network (WIN) Investment Club.

"Rather than looking at it as a club, they should look at it as a financial business they're entering into. Club members should be asking themselves, 'Is this a person we would want to be in business with 20 years from now?' You may have a friend who is a lot of fun, which is great for a club, but she also isn't one to follow through on things, which isn't so great for a business."[14]

Before moving on, O'Hara and Janke remind us, "In the final analysis, investment club members need only be individuals willing to work to gain knowledge, with an above-average desire to learn for themselves about the world of securities. Members should also regard their investment program as a lifelong process. Investing experience is not a requirement for success, as hundreds of high-performance NAIC clubs can attest."[15]

When Do I Meet With Them?

You've made all the right moves so far. You're ready now to proceed to the first real step: holding a meeting to determine which of the people on your list share your desire for education, profit and fun. This is the organizational meeting or, depending on which other books you may read, the exploratory, get-acquainted, initial, introductory, preparatory, preliminary or recruitment meeting. Fortunately, we all agree on the content of the meeting if not the name.

The Organizational Meeting

In actuality, you'll be holding two, maybe three of these get-togethers before truly inaugurating your club.

About two weeks prior to the first one, decide on a place and time. A home will do, but a public place such as a library conference room may be better to put everyone at ease, especially those who don't know the homeowner. Ask a few of the invitees whether they prefer a weeknight, a weekend morning or a weekend afternoon. Make it clear to all that the membership will eventually determine the preferred time for regular meetings, so as not to dissuade someone whose favorite TV show is on during the time you selected for the organizational meeting. Allow two hours for each of the initial meetings.

Now you'll want to send out invitations. A sample is shown in Figure 3-07. Along with the invitation, it's been proven effective to enclose a package of basic information to prepare prospective charter members for what they're getting into. The package can consist of any or all of the following:

SAMPLE OF INVITATION LETTER TO CLUB ORGANIZATIONAL MEETING

Date: Wednesday, October 20, 200x

Time: 7:00 PM

Place: Oakwood Library – Meeting room

Topic: Potential Start-up of an Investment Club

Dear   :

As we discussed a few days ago, a group of our neighbors are planning a "get-acquainted" meeting to discuss the idea of starting an investment club. You are invited to attend this informal meeting to discuss:

1. An overview of the pluses and minuses of an investment club
2. The types and amounts of work involved by investment club members
3. The club's investing philosophy
4. The overall reasonable expectations of forming an investment club
5. The planning process for forming an investment club
6. Questions and answers session

Please join us to see whether an investment club is right for you.

Refreshments will be served at the break.

See you on October 20th.

Sincerely,

John Smith, club organizer

FIGURE 3-07: SAMPLE INVITATION TO CLUB ORGANIZATIONAL MEETING

1. The Introduction and Chapter 1 of this book.

2. The NAIC sample partnership agreement and a sample of club operating procedures (see Chapter 4) clarifying member requirements and expectations.

3. A brief description of an investment club.

4. A disclaimer stating that there is risk involved, that there are no guarantees of any specific rates of return, and that investment clubs which follow NAIC principles are designed for long-term investing strategies. Add that many clubs of this type experience small gains or losses during the first year or two of operation.

It may appear that this is all designed to turn people off to the idea of an investment club rather than the other way around. Darn right. Better to weed out those who won't be productive members now than later. Those who do show up are demonstrating the kind of enthusiasm you'll be counting on for years to come.

CAUTION: prospective members will show up not only with enthusiasm but also with questions. If you're unqualified to respond, this is not the time for the blind to lead the blind. Attend an NAIC chapter meeting or seminar to make contact with experienced

club members, and ask one to help you conduct your organizational meeting. In some cases, the local NAIC chapter volunteers will make a "club visit" to help your club. Or, contact another NAIC-affiliated club and follow the same procedure.

Here are suggested agendas for the first and second organizational meetings. (Ask someone to take minutes, stressing that they are not volunteering to be the club's permanent secretary.)

The First Organizational Meeting.

1. Call the meeting to order. Note that this formal greeting is preferred to a cheery "Hi." It establishes that the club is a business first.

2. Introduce yourself and any NAIC member-guests who will be helping out. Give any pertinent data about yourselves (occupation, investing experience, NAIC-related experience, etc.).

3. Guest introductions. Break the ice by having each person introduce him or herself along with similar personal information as above.

4. Review the packet of information sent out with invitations—thereby defining the purpose of the meeting—and distribute/review the agenda. Mention also that one or two additional meetings will be necessary before the club is truly launched.

5. Explain in further detail what an investment club is and the benefits it provides. Introduce NAIC's four principles and solicit an understanding that the club will be subscribing to them. This is the place to also stress the disclaimers noted above. Introduce the three goals of investment clubs—education, profit and fun—and don't put undue emphasis on the middle one.

6. Hand out and give an overview of the NAIC sample partnership agreement and operating procedures. The purpose of doing so here is to demonstrate that the club will be following a long line of established clubs with real legal standing and proven procedures. It also clearly sets forth member obligations and responsibilities.

7. Open the floor for questions.

8. Take a break. Ten to fifteen minutes should do it. Let people talk amongst themselves without your doing too much mingling, as this may create some pressure on those unsure of whether to continue. That said, you may want to make the rounds in your friendliest manner, and offer those who plainly are not interested the chance to leave early with no hard feelings.

9. Following the break, ask once again if there are any questions on what has been covered thus far. As the next step is critical, be certain that everyone understands the nature of the beast. Give people a chance to express their own personal thoughts on what they think an investment club should be all about.

   If someone feels that the more conservative

buy-and-hold strategy advocated by NAIC is not for them, there's no sense in bringing them in kicking and screaming; they're bound to leave the same way, and soon. In reference to different investment approaches, you might say, "That's what makes horse races. However, the NAIC way to pick 'em has finished in the money for over fifty years."

10. Discuss the feasibility of the club and then determine how many guests are interested in pursuing their charter membership.

11. Announce that a second meeting will be necessary and go over the agenda. The organizational and task management abilities you show by doing this will give your guests confidence in the entire project. Set a time and place for the meeting. Perhaps this next one can be at someone's home with each person bringing a dish to pass. One week later is recommended; any longer lets the enthusiasm you've built up wane.

12. Assign some small tasks to prepare for the follow-up meeting. These include researching banks and

brokerages and looking into alternate partnership agreements and operations procedures. Recommend that volunteers access the NAIC Web Site (www.better-investing.org).

13. Ask everyone to come back with three possible names for the club. It's like having your own vanity license plate, so be creative.

14. Adjourn the meeting on a high note. Thank attendees for coming and congratulate them on taking the first step toward achieving the goals of "their" club. Have each person fill in his or her name, street address,

phone number and e-mail address on a sign-in sheet on the way out. This form should also have an area for each guest to suggest other people who might be interested and who should be invited to the second meeting. Allow guests to hang around as long as the meeting place is available or until the homeowner plugs in the vacuum.

With the completion of this first organizational meeting, you now know where you stand. A core of interested prospects has been assembled, and perhaps they've even given you some good direction and comments as well.

The second meeting will seek to review general items from the first for new attendees, followed by a more intense discussion and resolution of topics that are necessary for the legal establishment of the organization.

Here is a suggested agenda (once again, have someone volunteer to take minutes):

The Second Organizational Meeting.

1. Call the meeting to order. Welcome back returnees and new guests. Introduce yourself and any NAIC member-guests.

2. Call on new guests to introduce themselves first, followed by those who attended the first meeting.

3. Review items from the previous meeting: the purpose and benefits of an investment club, and the sample partnership agreement and operations procedures. (If no new guests are present, #2 and #3 can be skipped).

4. Distribute and review the agenda.

5. At this point, you may want to open the floor for questions, followed by a short break. Returnees may have inquiries they've been mulling over, and of course new guests will probably have some, too.

The balance of this meeting will be based on the assumption that everybody there is now committed to the establishment of the club and to the NAIC principles guiding it. Therefore, you may consider taking a break to allow new guests who want to opt out to do so—again, with no hard feelings.

6. The first order of business now is to choose a name. Remember the hit song by Johnny Cash, "A Boy Named Sue"? Unfortunately, Sue had no control over his nom de chanson. How delightful to have a little say in the naming of your very own club.

   If everyone did his or her homework, you now have a few dozen names from which to choose. This is your first discussion and vote, so make it a good one. Some names are strictly from Squaresville—for example, The (insert name of club president's home street) Investors Club. Others are way out there and mean something only to its members—Houston's BBCG Investment Club is composed of a "Bunch of Baptist Church Guys."

   Many clubs work hard to find a logical acronym—such as Women's Investment Club of Kalamazoo Earning Dollars (WICKED). Others leave little to chance—such the Filthy Rich Investors of Huntington, West Virginia.

   As we say, make it a good one; you all have to live with it. The club should actually come up with a short list of finalists, in case the first choice is taken. Contact your county clerk's office before registering to see if another club within the jurisdiction beat you to it.

7. Next on the agenda is to hear from those volunteers who took on the research of brokerages and banks. Brokers these days come in three flavors: full-service, discount and online. You'll also discuss the benefits of fee vs. non-fee bank accounts. (The entire subject will be discussed in Chapter 7).

8. Ask for a report on various partnership agreements and operating procedures as drafted by fellow members in the preceding week. (We'll do the same in Chapter 4). Discuss both documents as fully as time allows, but realize that you probably won't finalize them at this meeting.

9. You've covered a lot of ground. Remind members what's still to come in the meeting, especially the all-important election of officers. Take a short break for last-minute campaigning.

10. Come back from the break by reviewing in detail the obligations of members and officers (See Chapter 5). A good portion of this subject may have been discussed already in the examination of sample operating procedures.

11. Elect officers.

12. Hand out and discuss an estimated budget for initial

fees (See Figure 3-08). At this time, you may also decide on the minimum amount of regular monthly contributions. Some clubs set a $20 minimum amount, others $50, others more. You'll learn about "unit valuations" and NAIC club accounting in Chapter 6.

13. If the partnership agreement and/or operating procedures have not been completed, set up another meeting no more than one week later to do so. Once they are drafted, present them to the membership for ratification.

Then, decide on a day, time and place for regular monthly meetings. Some clubs prefer to rotate homes. Others eschew this as being too casual, favoring a meeting room at the library, a member's place of business, a community center or even a back room at a restaurant. (Investigate rental fees, which could be a factor in your decision.)

NOTE: NAIC club membership includes club liability insurance, which is often required at public meeting places. A copy of the liability insurance is included in the NAIC club welcome kit.

Clubs composed of people in the same company may vote to meet directly before or after work hours. Most clubs find that early evening works best. Be sure and specify a day of the week (e.g. the third Wednesday of the month) rather than a date (e.g. January 15). January 15, 2003 is, in fact, the third Wednesday of the month. February 15 and March 15, however, fall on Saturdays, which may be problematic.

Finally, discuss putting a clause in your operating procedures concerning attendance and penalties for missing meetings. Remember that this is a business in which one member's behavior affects all.

14. Meeting adjourned.

Congratulations. You now have yourself an investment club. Let the learning, the profit making and the fun begin!

FIGURE 3-08: INVESTMENT CLUB START-UP EXPENSES

Club start-up expenses will vary depending on state legal requirements and fees as well as membership decisions regarding discretionary funds and educational materials purchased. The following figures are for illustration purposes only.

CLUB EXPENDITURES

(Split equally between members)	In Dollars ($)
NAIC Club Membership	40
NAIC Club Accounting Software	169
(the online version = $49)	
Registration Fee with local & state govt.	40
Office Supplies/Photocopies	50
Phone/Fax/Postage	75
NAIC Materials (books, videos, tools)	125
Miscellaneous	35
Total	**534**

INDIVIDUAL EXPENDITURES

NAIC Membership	25
NAIC Online Premium Services	25
NAIC Stock Selection Guide Software	79 – 199
NAIC Materials (books, videos, tools)	50

Prices effective as of July 2004 and subject to change.

Summary

The ten steps to starting your investment club:

1. Hold an initial meeting.
2. Find members.
3. Elect officers.
4. Research the partnership agreement.
5. Draft operating procedures.
6. Register the club with local, state and federal agencies.
7. Open bank and brokerage accounts.
8. Join NAIC
9. Start monthly meetings and educational programs.
10. Use NAIC resources.

NAIC Individual Membership by Gender: 66% Female, 34% Male. NAIC Investment Club Membership by Gender: 54% Female, 38% Mixed, 8% Male

Consider these characteristics of prospective members:

- **Individual Investing Knowledge.**
  Look for people not too far above or below your own level of experience.

- **Individual Expertise.**
  Each member will embody a lifetime of personal wisdom that's bound to make your whole club greater than the sum of its parts.

- **Individual Wealth.**
  It shouldn't matter.

- **Individual Commitment.**
  It matters a great deal. Solicit people who display traits in their everyday lives that are essential for the success of the club.

- **Individual Residence.**
  If members are spread out, it could affect meeting attendance.

Gender, age, ethnicity and relationship are determining factors in the composition of investment clubs. There are all-women's clubs, all-student clubs and all-family clubs, as well as clubs that are all African American, all Asian, all Indian, all Arab and clubs from practically any ethnic, racial, cultural or societal group you can name. Consider that the most successful clubs are composed of individuals from a variety of backgrounds and experiences.

In the final analysis, investment club members need only be individuals willing to work to gain knowledge, with an above-average desire to learn for themselves about the world of securities.

Two or three organizational meetings will be necessary to determine interest in forming the club and in laying the basic structural groundwork.

Chapter Notes

[1] Ilene Meade, "How to Start an Investment Club," NAIC Investor's School, 27 Aug. 2001.

[2] Thomas E. O'Hara and Kenneth S. Janke, Sr., *Starting and Running a Profitable Investment Club* (New York: Times Books, 1998) 169.

[3] Meade.

[4] O'Hara and Janke 161.

[5] O'Hara and Janke 162.

[6] Marsha Bertrand, *Getting Started in Investment Clubs* (New York: John Wiley & Sons, Inc., 2001) 20.

[7] Bertrand 21.

[8] Jeff Fox with Judy Thompson, "Future Millionaires," *Better Investing* April 2001: 62-63.

[9] Carolyn M. Brown, *The Millionaires' Club: How to Start and Run Your Own Investment Club—and Make Your Money Grow!* (New York: John Wiley & Sons, Inc., 2000) 9.

[10] *Better Investing* April 2001:10.

[11] Brown 4.

[12] Amy Rauch Neilson, "Investing for the Family," *Better Investing* December 2001: 36-37. All Betty Taylor quotes are taken from this article.

[13] Douglas Gerlach and Angele McQuade, *Investment Clubs for Dummies* (New York: Hungry Minds, Inc., 2002) 21.

[14] Amy Rauch-Neilson, "Clubs: Keeping It Together," *Better Investing* July 2001: 36.

[15] O'Hara and Janke 163.

Business and Legal Aspects

You've now got a bunch of people together, you've got a group name and you've got some leaders. That's great. Still, you're not much more than, well, a bunch of people with a name and leaders.

I see where this is going. We still need to establish ourselves in the eyes of the government.

If you want to buy securities, that would be a good thing. The good news is, it's a pretty simple thing.

But do we all need accounting degrees to start a club?

No. However, your club may want to include someone with an accounting background. It is not a prerequisite, but will be helpful with any basic legal and tax advice on the options your club will soon face.

In this chapter, we'll take you through the processes of structuring your club, completing your partnership agreement, registering your club and drafting the club's operating procedures. Following that, we'll throw in some tips on planning for and conducting your monthly meeting.

Choosing a Business Entity

To determine which type of legal "business entity" is best for you, carefully review the upside and downside of each one.

General Partnership.

Most clubs go with this option. Start-up and operation costs are low, and the tax advantages are unbeatable. The partnership itself does not pay taxes, but does file an informational return (Form 1065, to be presented in Chapter 6). Members pay taxes on their portion of club income or gains on their individual returns, regardless of whether they are still with the club or have withdrawn.

Each member of the club is a general partner. Legally, each of you assumes full responsibility for the dealings of the partnership as a whole. Sounds like the makings of a bad "B" movie with the evildoer fleeing to Rio holding a bag of small bills.

Fortunately, NAIC can document no cases of such abuse within its membership. The sample partnership agreement you'll find in Figure 4-01 stipulates acceptable and unacceptable actions on the part of the partners.

In conjunction with the Securities Transfer Association, NAIC helped establish Rule 3.0610, which lets partnerships transfer securities using one authorized signature.

Normally, there is no need for any supporting papers. If your brokerage firm asks for supporting papers for all partners' signatures for transactions, refer it to the above rule number. Endorsement of your security certificates should read, "ABC Investment Club, a partnership, Jane Any Member, partner."

In order to monitor and help protect against any member misusing club funds, you should circulate the brokerage firm's monthly statement at every club meeting. Be sure you verify that each month's payments have been deposited to the account, that no unauthorized disbursements have been made, and that securities ordered have been purchased. The club should set a policy that the financial partner is to circulate the broker's most recent monthly account statement to all members at each monthly meeting.

Professor Perry Wallace of the American University School of Law in Washington, DC, notes that, for the average club, the partnership is customary since the members basically will be investing in stocks and bonds. They aren't doing anything speculative or highly creative to generate any liabilities.[1]

Consult your county clerk or state treasurer's office for specifics on your state's registration procedures, including the filing of the "Certificate of Conducting Business as Partners" or "Doing Business As (DBA)" form.

Limited Partnership.

With this form of partnership, you create two levels of ownership. In a limited partnership, a general partner (the members) may own no more than 20 percent of all the general partnership units. Both limited and general partners are unrestricted in their ownership of limited partnership units.

A limited partnership may be your choice if you plan to accept Individual Retirement Account funds as investment capital. In that case, the club must have a bona fide custodian as a member. In other words, a bank or brokerage house must be a limited partner serving as the IRA trustee, with no voice in the management of the club. Working members, as noted, are named general partners.

It's not complicated to set up and you can change from a general partnership to a limited partnership later at the club's discretion.

This is exactly what the Mutual Investment Club of Detroit did. After more than 40 years of operating with its original agreement (Figure 4-01), Mutual became a limited partnership in 1982 (Figure 4-03).

Limited Liability Partnership.

The limited liability partnership (LLP) was created to protect partners from that one guy heading down to Rio with the bag of bills and leaving them holding the bag for everything else. As the name implies,

partners would, in such case, incur limited liability for another member's actions. (Disclaimer: do not construe this paragraph as legal example or advice. Please consult your attorney to determine the scope of each person's personal liability in your specific situation.)

Tax filing procedures are the same as with the general and limited partnerships.

LLPs, however, may turn you off due to the cost of filing fees and drawing up the proper papers. In addition, not all states recognize uniform rules for this type of partnership. There are also annual renewal fees. While not prohibitive,

these administrative items complicate things a bit. You should weigh the increased protection from liability against the increased administrative costs and consider all this in light of Professor Wallace's statement regarding risk in the General Partnership section.

Corporation.

Setting up a corporation can be more complex and more expensive than forming a partnership. However, there are some advantages of a corporation vs. partnership that may make it an attractive alternative.

The two most common corporate entities are the "S" and "C" types. Each type is owned by its shareholders, to whom stock is issued.

With a "C" corporation, there is no limit on the number of people who may own shares. The SEC limits a partnership (which includes most investment clubs) to 99 members, unless it registers as an investment company. If your club has 100 or more members, consider

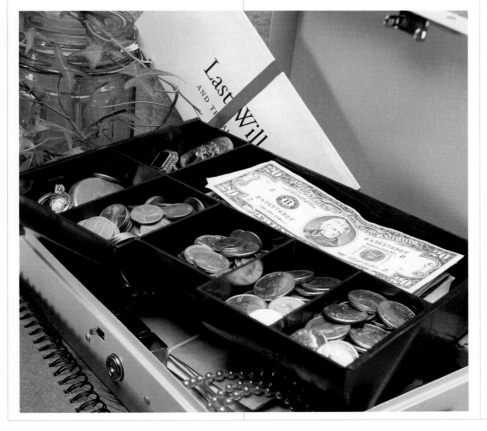

incorporating. Yes, some clubs do have that number, especially when set up to include as many employees of a large company who want to join.

NOTE: In NAIC's experience, clubs with more than 25 members are too cumbersome, making it difficult to manage monthly meetings.

The "C" Corp. also offers liability protection to its members. But you must balance that hypothetical possibility with the reality that "Cs" are double taxed. That is, the corporation (which is you, remember) pays taxes on gains and income. Any of these funds that are paid out to shareholders are deemed taxable income on personal returns, as well. That's two taxes on the same dollars. Gives you something to think about, eh?

The "S" corporation, on the other hand, offers the same tax treatment as an LLP—for federal taxes only, not state—but with the same set-up expense of the "C" corporation. The "S" is limited in most states to no more than 75 U.S. citizens-shareholders who must, in turn, reside in the same state (which would eliminate it from consideration for multi-state memberships).

Limited Liability Company.

An investment club wishing to obtain the liability protection of a corporation and tax advantages of a partnership may consider forming as a limited liability company (LLC). It can be taxed the same as a partnership, with any distributed income paid on members' returns at their personal tax rate.

The LLC is a relatively new form of entity and is not as familiar to most investors as a partnership. However, because it offers the best of both worlds – limited liability protection and partnership taxation, it may be the preferred entity for the future.

OK, look: for right now, just tell me which of these business entities is best for a little bitty group of people who just want to get together, learn about investing and make some money. We're not worrying about one of us skipping to Rio, and we don't have a whole lot to tie up in start-up and maintenance costs.

The Mutual Investment Club of Detroit reviewed partnership tax law and concluded that even with some of the advantages of being a corporation, only a partnership avoided paying two taxes on the same income. The members agreed that their tax obligations would be lower if the club operated as a partnership rather than as a corporation. In regards to personal liability, club members were satisfied that risk was minimal due to conducting only one business activity (buying/selling securities) and having only one party in its transactions (its broker).

The Partnership Agreement

The Mutual Investment Club has held up over the years—indeed, over the decades—and so has its charter Partnership Agreement, which is still used by NAIC as a template for new clubs.

What exactly is a partnership agreement, and how is it different from the club's operating procedures?

The partnership agreement is the founding blueprint that lays out the club's general purpose, objectives and specifications. The operating procedures are the guidelines that describe the club's everyday rules and regulations.

The partnership agreement is like a birth certificate; you won't have to produce it often, but it's invaluable to have around when you need it. The operating procedures are like a driver's license; you'll want it close-by constantly to help you get where you want to go.

The agreements developed by the Mutual Investment Club of Detroit are only examples and should not be considered legal or tax advice. In the case of the original agreement, copies were given to the SEC, the fifty state security commissions, the Internal Revenue Service, the Securities Transfer Association and the major securities industry exchanges and associations. None of these agencies expressed an opinion on the agreement.

Here now, in Figure 4-01, is that very 1940 document of the Mutual Investment Club of Detroit. Following that, in Figure 4-02, is a commentary to give some clarification to individual paragraphs. Figure 4-03 shows how the club revised its original agreement to a limited partnership in 1982.

NOTE: New investment clubs that join NAIC typically adopt and use the General Partnership Agreement shown below. However, because each investment club is different, you should consider consulting an attorney to determine if the General Partnership Agreement shown below will work for your investment club. After the first year, the club should review the agreement and decide if any changes are necessary.

PARTNERSHIP AGREEMENT OF THE MUTUAL INVESTMENT CLUB OF DETROIT

This AGREEMENT of PARTNERSHIP, effective as of _____ (date) by and between the undersigned, to wit:

(Names of partners)

NOW, THEREFORE IT IS AGREED:

1. **Formation.** The undersigned hereby form a General Partnership in accordance with and subject to the laws of the State of Michigan.

2. **Name.** The name of the partnership shall be Mutual Investment Club of Detroit.

3. **Term.** The partnership shall begin on _____ (date) and shall continue until December 31 of the same year and thereafter from year to year unless earlier terminated as hereinafter provided.

4. **Purpose.** The only purpose of the partnership is to invest the assets of the partnership solely in stocks, bonds and other securities ("securities") for the education and benefit of the partners.

5. **Meetings.** Periodic meetings shall be held as determined by the partnership.

6. **Capital Contributions.** The partners may make capital contributions to the partnership on the date of each periodic meeting in such amounts as the partnership shall determine, provided, however, that no partner's capital account shall exceed twenty percent (20%) of the capital accounts of all partners.

7. **Value of the Partnership.** The current value of the assets of the partnership, less the current value of the liabilities of the partnership, (hereinafter referred to as the "value of the partnership") shall be determined as of a regularly scheduled date and time ("valuation date") preceding the date of each periodic meeting determined by the Club.

8. **Capital Accounts.** A capital account shall be maintained in the name of each partner. Any increase or decrease in the value of the partnership on any valuation date shall be credited or debited, respectively, to each partner's capital account on that date. Any other method of valuating each partner's capital account may be substituted for this method, provided the substituted method results in exactly the same valuation as previously provided herein. Each partner's contribution to, or capital withdrawal from, the partnership shall be credited, or debited, respectively, to that partner's capital account.

9. **Management.** Each partner shall participate in the management and conduct of the affairs of the partnership in proportion to his capital account. Except as otherwise determined, all decisions shall be made by the partners whose capital accounts total a majority of the value of the capital accounts of all the partners.

10. **Sharing of Profits and Losses.** Net profits and losses of the partnership shall inure to, and be borne by, the partners, in proportion to the value of each of their capital accounts.

11. **Books of Account.** Books of account of the transactions of the partnership shall be kept and at all times be available and open to inspection and examination by any partner.

12. **Annual Accounting.** Each calendar year, a full and complete account of the condition of the partnership shall be made to the partners.

FIGURE 4-01: PARTNERSHIP AGREEMENT—PAGE 1 OF 3

13. **Bank Account.** The partnership may select a bank for the purpose of opening a bank account. Funds in the bank account shall be withdrawn by checks signed by any partner designated by the partnership.

14. **Broker Account.** None of the partners of this partnership shall be a broker. However, the partnership may select a broker and enter into such agreements with the broker as required for the purchase or sale of securities. Securities owned by the partnership shall be registered in the partnership name unless another name shall be designated by the partnership.

    Any corporation or transfer agent called upon to transfer any securities to or from the name of the partnership shall be entitled to rely on instructions or assignments signed by any partner without inquiry as to the authority of the person(s) signing such instructions or assignments, or as to the validity of any transfer to or from the name of the partnership.

    At the time of a transfer of securities, the corporation or transfer agent is entitled to assume (1) that the partnership is still in existence and (2) that this Agreement is in full force and effect and has not been amended unless the corporation has received written notice to the contrary.

15. **No Compensation.** No partner shall be compensated for services rendered to the partnership, except reimbursement for expenses.

16. **Additional Partners.** Additional partners may be admitted at any time, upon the unanimous consent of the partners, so long as the number of partners does not exceed twenty-five (25).

16A. **Transfers to a Trust.** A partner may, after giving written notice to the other partners, transfer his interest in the partnership to a revocable living trust of which he is the grantor and sole trustee.

16B. **Removal of a Partner.** Any partner may be removed by agreement of the partners whose capital accounts total a majority of the value of all partners' capital accounts. Written notice of a meeting where removal of a partner is to be considered shall include a specific reference to this matter. The removal shall become effective upon payment of the value of the removed partner's capital account, which shall be in accordance with the provisions on full withdrawal of a partner noted in paragraphs 18 and 20. The vote action shall be treated as receipt of request for withdrawal.

17. **Termination of Partnership.** The partnership may be terminated by agreement of the partners whose capital accounts total a majority in value of the capital accounts of all the partners. Written notice of a meeting where termination of the partnership is to be considered shall include a specific reference to this matter. The partnership shall terminate upon a majority vote of all partners' capital accounts. Written notice of the decision to terminate the partnership shall be given to all the partners. Payment shall then be made of all the liabilities of the partnership and a final distribution of the remaining assets either in cash or in kind, shall promptly be made to the partners or their personal representatives in proportion to each partner's capital account.

18. **Voluntary Withdrawal (Partial or Full) of a Partner.** Any partner may withdraw a part or all of the value of his capital account in the partnership and the partnership shall continue as a taxable entity. The partner withdrawing a part or all of the value of his capital account shall give notice of such intention in writing to the Secretary. Written notice shall be deemed to be received as of the first meeting of the partnership at which it is presented. If written notice is received between meetings it will be treated as received at the first following meeting.

    In making payment, the value of the partnership as set forth in the valuation statement prepared for the first meeting following the meeting at which notice is received from a partner requesting a partial or full withdrawal, will be used to determine the value of the partner's account.

    The partnership shall pay the partner who is withdrawing a portion or all of the value of his capital account in the partnership in accordance with paragraph 20 of this Agreement.

FIGURE 4-01: PARTNERSHIP AGREEMENT—PAGE 2 OF 3

19. **Death or Incapacity of a Partner.** In the event of the death or incapacity of a partner (or the death or incapacity of the grantor and sole trustee of a revocable living trust, if such trust is partner pursuant to Paragraph 16A hereof), receipt of notice shall be treated as a notice of full withdrawal.

20. **Terms of Payment.** In the case of a partial withdrawal, payment may be made in cash or securities of the partnership or a mix of each at the option of the partner making the partial withdrawal. In the case of a full withdrawal, payment may be made in cash or securities or a mix of each at the option of the remaining partners. In either case, where securities are to be distributed, the remaining partners select the securities.

Where cash is transferred, the partnership shall transfer to the partner (or other appropriate entity) withdrawing a portion or all of his interest in the partnership, an amount equal to the lesser of (i) ninety-seven percent (97%) of the value of the capital account being withdrawn, or (ii) the value of the capital account being withdrawn, less the actual cost to the partnership of selling securities to obtain cash to meet the withdrawal. The amount being withdrawn shall be paid within 10 days after the valuation date used in determining the withdrawal amount.

If the partner withdrawing a portion or all of the value of his capital account in the partnership desires an immediate payment in cash, the partnership at its earliest convenience may pay eighty percent (80%) of the estimated value of his capital account and settle the balance in accordance with the valuation and payment procedures set forth in paragraphs 18 and 20.

Where securities are transferred, the partnership shall select securities to transfer equal to the value of the capital account or a portion of the capital account being withdrawn (i.e., without a reduction for broker commissions). Securities shall be transferred as of the date of the club's valuation statement prepared to determine the value of that partner's capital account in the partnership. The Club's broker shall be advised that ownership of the securities has been transferred to the partner as of the valuation date used for the withdrawal.

21. **Forbidden Acts.** No partner shall:

(a) Have the right or authority to bind or obligate the partnership to any extent whatsoever with regard to any matter outside the scope of the partnership purpose.

(b) Except as provided in paragraph 16A, without the unanimous consent of all the other partners, assign, transfer, pledge, mortgage or sell all or part of his interest in the partnership to any other partner or other person whomsoever, or enter into any agreement as the result of which any person or persons not a partner shall become interested with him in the partnership.

(c) Purchase an investment for the partnership where less than the full purchase price is paid for same.

(d) Use the partnership name, credit or property for other than partnership purposes.

(e) Do any act detrimental to the interests of the partnership or which would make it impossible to carry on the business or affairs of the partnership.

This Agreement of Partnership shall be binding upon the respective heirs, executors, administrators and personal representatives of the partners.

The partners have caused this Agreement of Partnership to be executed on the dates indicated below, effective as of the date indicated above.

Partners: (Signatures of partners)[2]

FIGURE 4-01: PARTNERSHIP AGREEMENT—PAGE 3 OF 3

60

COMMENTARY ON THE PARTNERSHIP AGREEMENT
OF THE MUTUAL INVESTMENT CLUB OF DETROIT

Paragraphs 1, 2 and 3: Self-explanatory.

Paragraph 4: The purpose of the club is strictly limited. An important reason for such limitations is to reduce the actual or apparent authority of any partner.

Paragraph 5: Most clubs meet regularly, such as on the first business day of each month or the third Thursday. Regularity makes it possible for members to plan schedules and avoid conflicting engagements.

Paragraph 6: Since dollar cost averaging is one of the basic investment principles followed by NAIC clubs, most partners make a regular capital contribution at each meeting. In the majority of new clubs, partners normally deposit the same amount. In older clubs, partners frequently deposit varying amounts. For the convenience of the treasurer, a valuation unit of $10 is selected, and partner deposits are usually required to be made in multiples of $10 to facilitate bookkeeping.

Many clubs start out under the assumption that the membership will remain constant and all members will continue to contribute the same amount. However, change is inevitable. From the outset, you should use a recording system flexible enough to provide for varying capital contributions. New members will be easier to attract if only a modest regular monthly payment is suggested or required. On the other hand, some clubs are concerned that one particular partner might become a majority owner. Commonly, clubs provide that no partner may add to his or her capital account beyond a certain percentage of the total (often 20%).

Paragraph 7: The assets of an investment club constantly fluctuate. New capital coming into the club must be valued in proportion to the value of the partnership at the time of deposit. Otherwise, the new funds would immediately acquire a value greater or less than existing funds, depending on the club's current worth. To help determine the value of new deposits, a Valuation Statement is prepared for each meeting. To provide adequate time for compiling this statement, a cutoff date well in advance of the meeting date (e.g., ten days, last business day of the previous month, etc.) should be determined. Calculations are made effective as of that date.

Paragraph 8: Self-explanatory.

Paragraph 9: Most clubs provide that members will have a voice in the club's operation in proportion to their financial commitment. Generally, the members with the greatest financial interest have been members longer, and they have more experience. An investment club is a business and, like other businesses, seems to function best when decision-making power relates to risk capital employed.

Paragraph 10: Under current federal tax law, if the partnership earnings and losses are distributed on other than a pro rata basis, serious tax consequences could result.

Paragraph 11: NAIC offers accounting help to clubs in both text and software forms.

FIGURE 4-02: COMMENTARY ON THE PARTNERSHIP AGREEMENT —PAGE 1 OF 3

Paragraph 13: Many clubs do not have a bank account but deposit all funds with the broker and usually invest the available funds each month. Some clubs have the financial partner maintain a separate personal account for the club.

Paragraph 14: Initially, the Mutual Investment Club of Detroit did not allow a broker to be a member of the club, but it has since changed this policy. Clubs generally restrict broker contact to one member, who calls for suggestions about stocks to study, and transmits buy and sell orders.

Paragraph 15: Self-explanatory.

Paragraph 16: In the experience of NAIC, the strongest clubs have between ten and twenty members.

Paragraph 16A: Placing investment club equity in a revocable living trust provides two primary advantages to members choosing this option: probate expenses are avoided and the assets in the trust are immediately available for use as designated in the trust document.

Paragraph 16B: Sometimes a member loses interest in the club, consistently missing meetings and not doing his or her share of the work. Such a member will often just resign, so this paragraph's provision is seldom used.

Paragraph 17: Self-explanatory.

Paragraph 18: See Internal Revenue Code, Section 708 for further information on the continuation of a partnership as a taxable entity.

Paragraph 19: Same procedure as in paragraph 18 and paragraph 20. The remaining partners should exercise care to ensure that the deceased or incapacitated partner's account is paid in cash or stock to the proper claimant. Many clubs provide for the deposit of the deceased or incapacitated partner's funds in a separate bank account in cash, or to a brokerage account in stock, until advice is received as to ownership. An attorney can be consulted if there is any doubt about to whom payment should be made.

Paragraph 20: When a partner withdraws only part of the value of his or her capital account in the partnership, the partner has the choice of whether to receive cash or securities or a mix of the two.

Most partners seeking a partial withdrawal will choose to receive cash rather than securities since the tax consequences will usually be more favorable that way (see the following paragraph for further explanation). If cash is requested, the partnership must sell enough securities to satisfy the request and allocate any capital gain to all the partners in the current year. The partner withdrawing a portion of the capital account then reduces his or her tax basis by the amount of the cash distribution. If the partner has used up his or her tax basis, the distribution is then considered taxable income.

FIGURE 4-02: COMMENTARY ON THE PARTNERSHIP AGREEMENT —PAGE 2 OF 3

If the partner in a partial withdrawal chooses to receive securities, the club transfers securities of its choosing with a current value equal to the value being withdrawn. Any subsequent sale is at the discretion and expense of that partner. If the partner receives securities, under current federal tax law the partner withdrawing a portion of the value of his or her capital account is subject to federal income tax on the difference between the partnership's tax basis in the securities withdrawn and the value of the securities, but only on the partially withdrawing partner's subsequent sale of the securities on the open market.

When a partner requests full withdrawal of the entire value of his or her capital account in the partnership, the remaining members have the choice of satisfying the request in cash or securities or a mix of the two. If they choose to transfer cash, they must decide which securities to sell, divide any capital gain among all the partners, and then transfer the cash. The withdrawing partner recognizes a pro rata share of taxable income before the distribution. After the distribution, the withdrawing partner allocates his or her tax basis to the securities received in proportion to their value. Tax between the tax basis distributed on their receipt and the eventual sale is payable at the time of sale.

For the most benefit to remaining members, payment should be made by transferring securities with a substantial paper profit to the withdrawing partner. Currently, the Internal Revenue Code does not classify such a transfer as a taxable transaction, so the remaining members do not incur taxable income as they would if the securities were sold and cash paid to the withdrawing partner. The withdrawing partner will not have a taxable transaction if the securities are held, but once they are sold, he/she will have to recognize a taxable capital gain of the difference between the net selling price of the securities and his/her adjusted tax basis in the partnership assigned to the stock.

Transferring securities allows your club to postpone taxes on securities with capital gains while not increasing the tax liability of the withdrawing partner. Prior to the withdrawal date, that partner might consider opening an account with the same broker who handles the club's account. The securities can then be transferred and sold in the member's account on the same day, ensuring that he/she receives the current price.

Transaction costs (mainly broker commissions) may run as high as 10 percent in smaller clubs, while in larger clubs they may amount to only 3 percent or even less. When cash is distributed in a partial withdrawal, brokerage commissions as incurred (or 3 percent, whichever is the larger amount) are charged to the partially withdrawing partner, and the net proceeds are then distributed to that partner. Because securities fluctuate in value, the date used to determine the partner's capital account value should be set after the date of sale of securities used to satisfy the partner's request.

Paragraph 21: Self-explanatory.[3]

FIGURE 4-02: COMMENTARY ON THE PARTNERSHIP AGREEMENT —PAGE 3 OF 3

63

With the creation of the Individual Retirement Account (a federal income tax planning vehicle to defer tax on income), the Mutual Investment Club of Detroit sought a means of allowing members to invest their IRAs in the club. To accommodate IRA requirements, Mutual had to arrange for an approved IRA custodian (bank or trust company) to become a member of the club. Further regulations required that member to be a limited partner. Mutual became a limited partnership in 1982 after more than forty years of operating with its original agreement.

The trustee of an IRA account (typically a bank) may only be a limited partner, and therefore has no voice in the day to day management of the club.

When a partner wishes to establish an IRA account in the club, and the other members agree to it, the partnership agreement could be altered as shown below.

If a member has an IRA account in the club, he/she typically maintains a general partner account also. During the year members usually make deposits only to their general partner accounts. Since the trustee of the IRA account probably charges a fee for each transaction, members try to limit the number of transactions they make in IRA accounts. Some accumulate cash and make only one IRA deposit per year. Others make deposits into their general partner account and transfer funds to the IRA or account annually.

LIMITED PARTNERSHIP AGREEMENT
OF MUTUAL INVESTMENT CLUB
OF DETROIT LIMITED PARTNERSHIP

THIS AGREEMENT OF LIMITED PARTNERSHIP, effective (Date), by and between the undersigned as General Partners, to:

(Names of General Partners)

and (name) Bank, Trustee of the Individual Retirement Trust Accounts, Master Trust agreement.

(If the Club is a new partnership, it would begin at paragraph 1, below. If it is a Club converting from a general to a limited partnership, it should include wording appropriate to the law of its own State similar to the following, through "NOW THEREFORE, IT IS AGREED.")

WHEREAS, the Mutual Investment Club of Detroit has been in existence as a general partnership for over forty-six (46) years and has executed numerous partnership agreements based upon various changes in partners, but such partnership has continued as one tax entity since its formation; and

WHEREAS, the partners of the Mutual Investment Club of Detroit desire to organize such partnership as a limited partnership as such term is defined by the Michigan Revised Uniform Limited Partnership Act, MCL 449.1101 et seq. and, therefore, the partners desire and hereby do cancel the previous partnership agreement but continue as the same tax entity.

NOW, THEREFORE, IT IS AGREED:

1. **Formation.** The undersigned hereby form a Limited Partnership (the "partnership") in, and in accordance with the laws of the State of Michigan. All partners shall be general partners except those admitted to serve as Trustees of IRA Accounts on behalf of the general partners with such trustees to be referred to as "limited partners."

FIGURE 4-03: LIMITED PARTNERSHIP AGREEMENT—PAGE 1 OF 3

2. **Name.** The name of the partnership shall be: Mutual Investment Club of Detroit Limited Partnership.

(Paragraphs 3 through 5 of the preceding agreement would be unchanged)

6. **Capital Contributions.** The partners may make capital contributions to the partnership on the date of each periodic meeting in such amounts as the partnership shall determine, provided, however, that no general partner's capital account shall exceed twenty percent (20%) of the capital accounts of all the general partners.

(Paragraphs 7 and 8 of the preceding agreement would be unchanged)

9. **Management.** Each general partner shall participate in the management and conduct of the affairs of the partnership in proportion to the value of his capital account. Except as otherwise determined, all decisions shall be made by the general partners whose capital accounts total a majority of the value of the capital accounts of all the general partners.

(Paragraphs 10 through 15 of the preceding agreement would be unchanged.)

16. **Additional Partners.** Additional partners may be admitted at any time, upon the unanimous consent of all the general partners, so long as the number of general partners does not exceed twenty (20).

   By creating a limited partnership, club members are able to invest their IRAs and defer taxable income.

16A. **Transfers to a Trust.** A general partner may, after giving written notice to the other general partners, transfer his interest in the partnership to a revocable living trust of which he is the grantor and sole trustee.

16B. **Removal of a Partner.** Any partner may be removed by agreement of the general partners whose capital accounts total a majority of the value of all partners' capital accounts. Written notice of a meeting where removal of a partner is to be considered shall include a specific reference to this matter. The removal shall become effective upon payment of the value of the removed partner's capital account, which shall be in accordance with the provisions of full withdrawal of a partner noted in paragraphs 18 and 20.

16C. **Limited Partners.** If any general partner establishes an IRA (under section 408 of the Internal Revenue Code), the trustee of such account may be admitted to the Partnership as a limited partner. No limited partner shall have the obligation or the right to participate in the management of the Partnership or in Partnership decisions, and shall have no liability with respect to partnership obligations, and the provisions of this Agreement relating specifically to General Partners shall not apply to Limited Partners. No general partner may own more than 20% of the value of all the general partners' capital accounts. Both general and limited partners are unrestricted in their purchase of limited partnership units. Unless otherwise required by law, Limited Partners shall not be counted as partners in applying the limitation on the number of partners allowed under this Agreement. Limited partners shall not have the power to grant the right to become a limited partner to an assignee of any part of the partnership interest.

17. **Termination of Partnership.** The partnership may be terminated by agreement of the general partners whose capital accounts total a majority in value of the capital accounts of all the general partners. Written notice of the meeting where termination of the partnership is to be considered shall include a specific reference to this matter. The partnership shall terminate upon a majority vote of all general partners' capital accounts. Written notice of the decision to terminate the partnership shall be given to all the general partners. Payment shall then be made of all the liabilities of the general partnership and a final distribution of the remaining assets, either in cash or in kind, shall promptly be made to the general partners or their personal representatives in proportion to each general partner's capital account.

FIGURE 4-03: LIMITED PARTNERSHIP AGREEMENT—PAGE 2 OF 3

(Paragraph 18 of the preceding agreement would be unchanged.)

19. **Death or Incapacity of a General Partner.** In the event of the death or incapacity of a general partner (or the death or incapacity of the grantor and sole trustee of a revocable living trust, if such trust is a general partner pursuant of Paragraph 16A hereof), receipt of notice of such an event shall be treated as notice of full withdrawal.

(Continue with the preceding agreement to paragraph 21B and at the end add:) No limited partner shall have the power to assign, transfer, pledge, mortgage or sell all or part of his interest in the partnership.

(After paragraph 21e continue:)

This Agreement of Limited Partnership hereby declared and shall be binding upon the respective heirs, executors, trustees, administrators and personal representatives of the parties.

The parties have caused this Agreement of Limited Partnership to be executed on the dates indicated below, effective on the date indicated above.

Partners: (Signatures of General Partners)

Partners: (Signatures of Limited Partners)[4]

FIGURE 4-03: LIMITED PARTNERSHIP AGREEMENT—PAGE 3 OF 3

Registering the Club

Once you've selected the most appropriate business entity, you have to properly register the club with certain government agencies.

For a general partnership, file a "Certificate of Conducting Business as Partners" form, known as a "Doing Business As (DBA)" form with the county or state. Requirements vary, so have the club secretary or treasurer contact the Secretary of State's office or licensing board, as well as the office of your local county clerk. There may be minimal fees for some of the forms you'll file.

At this time you may find, however unlikely, that the club name you all agonized over for weeks is already being used. Go to Plan B.

Depending on the state, you may have a few more hurdles to clear. In Minnesota, for example, you'll have to publish an announcement of your club's formation in a newspaper originating in the county where your treasurer lives. This Certified Name announcement also needs to include the names of all club members.[5]

After the local and state honchos are happy, you'll now have to let one particular relative know about it.

Who's that?

Uncle Sam. He's finicky that way. He figures as long as you'll be taking in all those dividends and capital gains, he'd like to know where you are so he can cut himself in.

In short, your club—no matter what its business structure—will need to apply for an Employer Identification Number, or EIN. In addition to using this number for taxpaying purposes, you'll need it to open your bank and brokerage accounts and to purchase securities.

But how do they figure we're an employer?

Does it matter? Anyway, if you want to nitpick, go ahead and call it a Taxpayer Identification Number, or TIN. Same difference.

To apply for one, obtain and fill out IRS Form SS-4. Print it off their Web site (www.irs.gov) or pick one up at the library. The club will be assigned a nine-digit number that you'll need to include on your individual return as well if you're 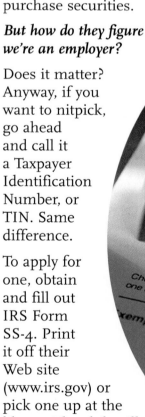 reporting any income or loss from your club transactions.

Figure 4-04 shows Form SS-4. After you submit the form, you'll receive your EIN in about four weeks. If you need it sooner to open a brokerage account, you can call the Tele-TIN phone number shown on the SS-4 Instructions. You will receive a number immediately. Enter the number in the upper right-hand corner of the SS-4 and send it in.

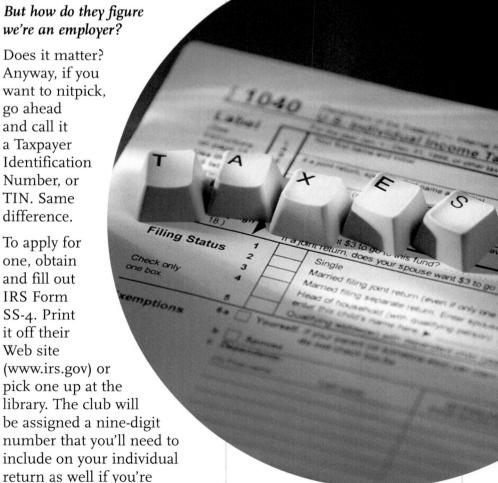

Form **SS-4**

(Rev. December 2001)

Department of the Treasury
Internal Revenue Service

Application for Employer Identification Number

(For use by employers, corporations, partnerships, trusts, estates, churches, government agencies, Indian tribal entities, certain individuals, and others.)

▶ See separate instructions for each line. ▶ Keep a copy for your records.

EIN

OMB No. 1545-0003

Type or print clearly.

1 Legal name of entity (or individual) for whom the EIN is being requested

2 Trade name of business (if different from name on line 1)

3 Executor, trustee, "care of" name

4a Mailing address (room, apt., suite no. and street, or P.O. box)

5a Street address (if different) (Do not enter a P.O. box.)

4b City, state, and ZIP code

5b City, state, and ZIP code

6 County and state where principal business is located

7a Name of principal officer, general partner, grantor, owner, or trustor

7b SSN, ITIN, or EIN

8a Type of entity (check only one box)

☐ Sole proprietor (SSN) _____
☐ Partnership
☐ Corporation (enter form number to be filed) ▶ _____
☐ Personal service corp.
☐ Church or church-controlled organization
☐ Other nonprofit organization (specify) ▶ _____
☐ Other (specify) ▶

☐ Estate (SSN of decedent) _____
☐ Plan administrator (SSN) _____
☐ Trust (SSN of grantor) _____
☐ National Guard   ☐ State/local government
☐ Farmers' cooperative   ☐ Federal government/military
☐ REMIC   ☐ Indian tribal governments/enterprises
Group Exemption Number (GEN) ▶ _____

8b If a corporation, name the state or foreign country (if applicable) where incorporated

State

Foreign country

9 Reason for applying (check only one box)
☐ Started new business (specify type) ▶_____
☐ Hired employees (Check the box and see line 12.)
☐ Compliance with IRS withholding regulations
☐ Other (specify) ▶

☐ Banking purpose (specify purpose) ▶ _____
☐ Changed type of organization (specify new type) ▶ _____
☐ Purchased going business
☐ Created a trust (specify type) ▶ _____
☐ Created a pension plan (specify type) ▶ _____

10 Date business started or acquired (month, day, year)

11 Closing month of accounting year

12 First date wages or annuities were paid or will be paid (month, day, year). **Note:** *If applicant is a withholding agent, enter date income will first be paid to nonresident alien. (month, day, year)* . . . . ▶

13 Highest number of employees expected in the next 12 months. **Note:** *If the applicant does not expect to have any employees during the period, enter ¡-0-.¡*

Agricultural	Household	Other

14 Check **one** box that best describes the principal activity of your business.
☐ Construction ☐ Rental & leasing ☐ Transportation & warehousing   ☐ Health care & social assistance ☐ Wholesale–agent/broker
☐ Real estate ☐ Manufacturing ☐ Finance & insurance   ☐ Accommodation & food service ☐ Wholesale–other ☐ Retail
☐ Other (specify)

15 Indicate principal line of merchandise sold; specific construction work done; products produced; or services provided.

16a Has the applicant ever applied for an employer identification number for this or any other business? . . . . ☐ **Yes** ☐ **No**
Note: *If ¡Yes,¡ please complete lines 16b and 16c.*

16b If you checked "Yes" on line 16a, give applicant's legal name and trade name shown on prior application if different from line 1 or 2 above.
Legal name ▶   Trade name ▶

16c Approximate date when, and city and state where, the application was filed. Enter previous employer identification number if known.
Approximate date when filed (mo., day, year)   City and state where filed   Previous EIN

Third Party Designee
Complete this section **only** if you want to authorize the named individual to receive the entity¡s EIN and answer questions about the completion of this form.
Designee's name   Designee's telephone number (include area code) ( )
Address and ZIP code   Designee's fax number (include area code) ( )

Under penalties of perjury, I declare that I have examined this application, and to the best of my knowledge and belief, it is true, correct, and complete.   Applicant's telephone number (include area code) ( )

Name and title (type or print clearly) ▶

Signature ▶   Date ▶   Applicant's fax number (include area code) ( )

For Privacy Act and Paperwork Reduction Act Notice, see separate instructions.   Cat. No. 16055N   Form **SS-4** (Rev. 12-2001)

FIGURE 4-04: FORM SS-4

The Operating Procedures

When Moses came down from the mountain, he carried Ten Commandments (fifteen if you believe Mel Brooks in the film *History of the World, Part I*). Your club can have as many as it wants. And interestingly enough, the forty days it allegedly took Moses to receive his laws is a reasonable time for you to come up with yours.

The operating procedures are the day-to-day rules by which the club is run. One difference between operating procedures and the partnership agreement is the durability of the respective documents. Once drafted and signed, you should consider the partnership agreement something to put with your important financial papers. It will then be taken out and revised only when the membership changes and it needs to be signed all over again, or in extraordinary cases when an amendment must be added.

Some advisors suggest revising the partnership agreement only once per year, and having new members sign a statement agreeing to abide by the partnership agreement in the interim.[6] A person leaving the club presents a more urgent need to pass the partnership agreement around once more.

The operating procedures, by contrast, are designed to

be more flexible. Perhaps somewhere down the line the club decides to change the day of the monthly meeting or increase the minimum investment. Such provisions do not alter the basic overall purpose or investment policies of the club.

Let's take a look at three samples of club operating procedures. Figure 4-05 is taken from the first minutes of the Mutual Investment Club of Detroit. The Dollars and Sense Investment Club, one of the three clubs that NAIC online instructor Ilene Meade belongs to in Minnesota, are using Figure 4-06 successfully. Figure 4-07 comes from the Triple E Investment Club in Colorado.

OPERATING PROCEDURES MUTUAL INVESTMENT CLUB

Duties of Partners

Annually, at the first meeting in February, partners shall elect the following positions and assign duties as described below by a majority vote:

1. **President.** The President's duty is to preside over meetings, set meeting dates and locations, appoint committees and see that resolutions passed by the partnership are carried out.

2. **Vice-President.** The Vice-President takes the place of the President when the President is absent or incapacitated. The Vice-President shall assign companies to report on at Club meetings to each partner and shall be responsible for insuring that the Club's study program is properly carried out.

3. **Secretary.** The Secretary's duty is to keep a record of the actions authorized by the partners and notify partners of meetings and other activities.

4. **Treasurer.** The Treasurer's duty is to keep a record of the Club's receipts and disbursements and partners' interests in the Club. The Treasurer will give partners receipts for payments, place the buy and sell orders authorized by the partners with the Club's broker, and prepare the Club's monthly valuation statement. He/she will see that the needed tax information is compiled and file the necessary reports.

Guests

Partners may invite guests to any meeting of the Club as long as advance clearance is obtained from the host of the meeting. When consideration is given to adding partners to the Club under paragraph 16 of the Club's partnership agreement, anyone considered shall have been a guest for at least two prior meetings.

Meetings

The Club shall hold a meeting on the second Tuesday of each month at a place designated by the Club. Written notice of each meeting shall be given to each partner by the Secretary at least one week before the meeting. Special meetings may be called by the President upon similar notice to the other partners.

Procedure

The monthly valuation statement shall be effective as of a regularly scheduled date and time preceding each monthly meeting.

In maintaining the records of each partner's capital account in the Club, the unit value method will be used.

Additional deposits in the Club may be made by members in multiples of $10.

The Vice-President shall contact investment counsel immediately preceding the monthly meeting and secure investment counsel's suggestions on new companies to consider, and any comments on stocks owned by the Club. He shall report this information at the meeting. The Vice-President shall appoint at least two partners at each meeting to prepare a report on the NAIC Stock Selection Guide on a security for presentation to the partnership at the following meeting. The Vice-President shall remind each person assigned to prepare a NAIC Stock Selection Guide of his assignment one week before the meeting.

Buy and/or sell action may be taken after a period of discussion by the members, and when voted by a simple majority of the members' interests.

End of motion.

FIGURE 4-05: OPERATING PROCEDURES MUTUAL INVESTMENT CLUB

OPERATING PROCEDURES DOLLARS AND SENSE INVESTMENT CLUB A GENERAL PARTNERSHIP

1. **FEES:** The initial fee of each partner will be one hundred dollars ($100) which goes to Petty Cash and Operating Revenues. The initial fee of $100 per partner does stay with the Club in the event of a partner's withdrawal from the Club.

2. **NEW MEMBERS:** A new member may initially contribute money up to the average of the balances in the existing individual accounts. "Time-based earnings" is the accounting method. The Club shall not exceed fifteen (15) partners.

3. **DUES & CONTRIBUTIONS:** Partner investment dues of twenty dollars ($20) minimum will be due at each monthly meeting. A partner may contribute additional deposits but cannot exceed limitation as set forth in Article 6, Capital Contributions, of the Partnership Agreement.

4. **ACCOUNTING METHOD:** Partners' shares are tracked as investment credit units. The amount is ten dollars ($10) for one unit.

5. **VOTING:** Decisions shall be made by a majority of partners (each partner has one written vote) unless a request is made for a vote based on proportional ownership.

6. **OFFICERS:** The President, Vice-President, Secretary, and the Treasurer shall be elected annually during the regular November meeting. (The Treasurer may have an Assistant to the Treasurer—a volunteer or be appointed.) The newly elected officers shall assume the duties of their respective offices at the following January meeting of each year. Officer's terms will be for a one-year period. Officers may succeed themselves in the same office.

7. **DUTIES OF OFFICERS:** The duties of the officers are:

A. **PRESIDENT:** The duties of the President shall be to preside at meetings, set meeting dates and locations, appoint committees, and see that resolutions passed by the partnership are carried out.

B. **VICE-PRESIDENT:** The Vice-President shall assume the duties of the President when the President is absent or temporarily unable to carry out his/her duties. In addition, the Vice-President may assign companies to report on at Club meetings to partners and shall be responsible for insuring that the Club's study program is properly carried out.

C. **SECRETARY:** The Secretary shall maintain the partnership records, keep record of the actions authorized by the partners and notify partners of meetings and other activities.

D. **TREASURER:** The Treasurer's duty is to keep a record of the Club's receipts and disbursements and partners' interests in the Club. The Treasurer will give partners receipts for their payments, place the buy and sell orders authorized by the partners with the Club's broker or National Association of Investors Corporation (NAIC) and prepare the Club's monthly valuation statement. The Treasurer will receive all correspondence for the Club and will forward the materials to the proper partner. The Treasurer will see that the needed tax information is compiled and file the necessary reports for Treasurer's term of office. Checks must be signed by two partners: Treasurer and another partner designated by the membership.

8. **ANNUAL AUDIT:** The Vice-President will appoint an audit committee consisting of two (2) or more of the general partners who are not signatories on the Partnership accounts. The audit will be completed within ninety (90) days of year-end.

9. **DESIGNATED MEETING:** Meetings will be held on the second Monday of each month at 7:00 PM. A majority of the general partners can change the meeting time.

NOTE: This information is provided only as an example to aid in understanding how a sample club can function. This club decided to modify the sample NAIC Partnership Agreement to meet the needs of its members.

FIGURE 4-06: OPERATING PROCEDURES DOLLARS AND SENSE INVESTMENT CLUB A GENERAL PARTNERSHIP

OPERATING PROCEDURES OF THE TRIPLE INVESTMENT CLUB

1. **FORMATION OF PARTNERSHIP:** Refer to Partnership Agreement.

2. **NAME OF PARTNERSHIP:** Refer to Partnership Agreement.

3. **TERM**: Refer to Partnership Agreement.

4. **PURPOSE**: To benefit partners, educationally and financially, by investing in securities, while employing fundamental principles and techniques of sound investment practices.

5. **MEETINGS** (Regular, Special, Quorum)

   a. Regular meetings of the Partnership shall be held on the 3rd Tuesday of every month. Meetings may be cancelled or rescheduled by a majority vote of all partners present in a quorum at a given meeting.

   b. Time of meeting shall be from 6:00 to 8:00 p.m.

   c. In the month of February, the annual meeting shall be held in conjunction with the regular business meeting at which time new officers will be elected and a full and complete annual accounting of the financial condition of the Partnership shall be made to the partners.

   d. Special meetings may be called at any time by the Presiding Partner. Also, any three (3) partners may request a special meeting through the Presiding Partner, in writing. In all cases, special meetings shall be limited to the stated purpose which must be communicated in advance to all partners.

   e. A quorum of eight (8) partners shall be present at any regular or special meeting in order for Partnership business to be conducted, e.g., buy or sell orders. A simple majority is needed to approve any Partnership business not otherwise specified in the Operating Procedures herein.

   f. A simple majority of the Partnership and shall be present at any regular, special, or annual meeting before the election of officers, amendments to the Partnership Agreement or Partnership Operating Procedures can commence. A simple majority of the partners present is needed to approve amendments to the Partnership Agreement, Operating Procedures, or elect officers.

   g. Each partner shall have one vote in all matters regardless of his capital account balance.*

   h. Any partner who fails to attend three (3) consecutive regular meetings and is not excused by the Presiding Partner from attending any such meetings, or six (6) meetings in any twelve- (12) month period, will be considered for termination.

6. **CONTRIBUTIONS**

   a. Assessments are made on a monthly basis and are due and payable on or before the date set for the monthly meeting. The same shall become delinquent five (5) days after the monthly meeting.

   b. The investment amount received from each partner shall be $25 monthly and an annual administrative fee of $25.

   c. Any partner who fails to make contributions to capital when they become due and payable, and who shall continue in default in the payment of such assessments for a period of sixty (60) days, shall, at the expiration of said sixty (60) days, be given notice by registered mail of this delinquency by the Presiding Partner; and if all delinquent payments be not paid within fifteen (15) days from date of mailing notice of delinquency, then said partner shall be automatically dropped from the Partnership rolls.

7. **VALUATION:** The closing stock exchange prices five (5) calendar days preceding each monthly meeting shall be used to determine the liquidating value of the club.

8. **CAPITAL ACCOUNTS:** Refer to Partnership Agreement.

9. **MANAGEMENT**

   a. Refer to Partnership Agreement.

   b. Voting to expel a partner from the Partnership shall be decided by simple majority vote of the partners present in a quorum required for such purpose.

   c. Voting to relieve a partner of her duties shall be decided by a simple majority vote of the partners present in a quorum required for such purpose.

   d. All voting to elect officers, to admit new partners, to expel partners or relieve officers of duties shall be conducted by secret ballot.

   e. For any other voting, a secret ballot may be called for by any one partner of the Partnership.

10. **SHARING OF PROFITS AND LOSSES:** Refer to Partnership Agreement

11. **BOOK OF ACCOUNT:** Shall be a complete set of accounts, consisting of assets, liabilities, individual Partnership accounts, appropriate revenue and expense accounts, using the double entry accounting system as prescribed in the NAIC Investment Club Accounting Handbook.

12. **ANNUAL ACCOUNTING**

   a. The annual accounting shall take place in February at the annual meeting, for the preceding year.

   b. All financial transactions shall be reviewed by a Partnership Audit Committee semi-annually.

13. **BANK ACCOUNT:** All checks shall be signed by either the Financial, Presiding or Assistant Presiding Partner unless check amount exceeds $500. Then two (2) signatures are required.

14. **BROKER ACCOUNT**

   a. All securities shall be purchased in the name of the Partnership.

   b. All securities shall be kept in the Partnership safe deposit box or with the broker. **

   c. The Presiding Partner and the Assistant Presiding Partner shall be the custodian of all securities.

15. **NO COMPENSATION:** Refer to Partnership Agreement.

16. **ADDITIONAL PARTNERS**

   a. Fourteen (14) partners formed the Partnership.

   b. A prospective partner must attend at least three (3) meetings as an observer. Membership must be requested in writing and may be submitted no earlier than at the third meeting that the candidate attends as an observer. At the end of the meeting at which a membership request is submitted, the prospective member will be excused from the meeting and the regular members will stay for an extra fifteen minutes in order to vote on the membership request.

c. A unanimous vote of the membership present in a quorum shall be required for admittance of a new partner.

d. All new partners are required to contribute a $25 administration fee and a capital contribution as set by the Partnership.

e. New members are required to attend the 10-hour NAIC course on preparing SSG's during the first nine (9) months of membership.

f. Prospective members must be sponsored/mentored by an existing member.

g. Any member who wishes to invite a prospective new member to a meeting shall notify the club prior to the candidate's first attendance as an observer.

17. **VOLUNTARY TERMINATION:** Refer to Partnership Agreement.

18. **WITHDRAWAL OF A PARTNER:** Refer to Partnership Agreement.

19. **DEATH OR INCAPACITY OF A PARTNER:** Refer to Partnership Agreement.

20. **PURCHASE PRICE**

a. Refer to Partnership Agreement.

b. The Partnership shall have three (3) weeks in which to complete the buy out.

21. **DUTIES OF PARTNERS**

Presiding Partner

a. Shall preside at all regular and special meetings of the Partnership and oversee all Partnership activities.

b. Shall ensure that all resolutions passed by the Partnership are carried out.

c. Shall appoint members to the Audit Committee.

d. Shall coordinate the research activities of the Partnership of which all partners are part.

e. Shall sign some checks issued against the Partnership checking account.

Assistant Presiding Partner

f. Shall take the place of the Presiding Partner when the Presiding Partner is absent or incapacitated.

g. Shall coordinate the portfolio management function of the Partnership for which all partners are responsible.

h. Shall keep a file of all stock selection reports made by the partners.

i. Shall coordinate the education program of the Partnership.

j. Shall sign some checks issued against the Partnership checking account.

Recording Partner

k. Shall keep minutes of all regular and special Partnership meetings.

l. Shall notify partners of regular and special meetings.

m. Shall keep a record of attendance for regular and special Partnership meetings.

n. Shall prepare agenda for regular and special Partnership meetings as directed by the Presiding Partner.

FIGURE 4-07: OPERATING PROCEDURES OF THE TRIPLE INVESTMENT CLUB—PAGE 3 OF 4

Financial Partner

o. Shall maintain a complete set of books.

p. Shall prepare and present a monthly statement of liquidating value at regular and special Partnership meetings.

q. Shall prepare the Partnership Tax/Information Return and notify all partners of their tax liability on the appropriate IRS forms.

r. Shall receive and deposit all receipts into the Partnership checking account and make most disbursements from the Partnership checking account.

s. Shall sign/countersign some checks issued against the Partnership checking account.

t. Shall prepare and present monthly bank reconciliation at regular and special Partnership meetings.

u. Shall act as Agent, placing all buy and sell orders authorized by the partners at regular or special Partnership meetings.

Partner

v. Shall pay monthly assessments in a timely manner.

w. Shall attend Partnership meetings on a regular basis.

x. Shall, from time to time, serve on the Partnership Audit Committee.

y. Shall participate in the stock selection and portfolio maintenance functions of the Partnership.

z. Shall participate in the Partnership education and research activities.

In Witness whereof, the partners have set their hand, the year and date stated below:

(Signatures of partners)

* NAIC has observed that after a club has been in existence for several years, certain members may build a significantly larger holding than others in the club. At this point the club may consider including an addition to the general partnership agreement stating that members with a determined higher percentage ownership in the club may have more votes than a person with substantially lower percentage ownership in the club.

** Most brokers require securities to be deposited with them.

NOTE: This information is provided only as an example to aid in understanding how a sample club can function. This club decided to modify the sample NAIC Partnership Agreement to meet the needs of its members.

FIGURE 4-07: OPERATING PROCEDURES OF THE TRIPLE INVESTMENT CLUB—PAGE 4 OF 4

There are numerous differences in the three documents. Most obvious is the length. In patterning themselves after the original Mutual Operating Procedures, D&S covers all it wants to say in nine clauses. Triple E—which, by the way, stands for Education, Enjoyment and Enrichment—includes 21 clauses in its list.

Mutual and D&S name its officers president, vice-president, secretary and treasurer. Triple E goes for presiding partner, assistant presiding partner, recording partner and financial partner, and also adds duties of the members (partners) themselves.

Mutual and D&S stipulate the time and day of its meetings in a few sentences. Triple E provides not only for regular and special meetings, but also necessary quorums, voting specifications and cause for termination due to absenteeism.

You should read each document carefully and note the other differences.

So of the three, which one is better?

There is no better or worse. Your club can learn from each of these efforts, but in the end it comes down to what works best for all of you. Is Triple E too restrictive? Or, is it simply getting everything in writing now, planning for any eventuality and not leaving anything to

interpretation later? Let's face it, you don't want members missing multiple meetings or contributions and then crying, "I didn't know" when they're asked to leave.

It's important to remember why you opened shop in the first place and the benefits of team investing. If someone is in arrears with a monthly contribution, it's not just that person who loses out. The pool of money is lowered, fewer shares are purchased and the total return will be affected proportionately. Everybody loses.

There's another consideration, perhaps more serious. If enough people miss enough meetings, it creates a passive membership. The Internal Revenue Service (IRS) can rule that the active members, by virtue of their buying and selling securities for the entire club, are then the de facto custodians or directors of an organization operating as a corporation, and thus taxable as such. You really don't want to go there.

You may ask your NAIC Chapter for examples of operating procedures from other clubs. And again, consider your own document a work in progress. It's like spending time at the shoe store; keep trying 'em on until you get one that fits just right.

The Monthly Meeting

NAIC is not NASA. Despite all your well-intentioned efforts to conduct the club as a lean, mean, money-making machine, it's not always going to work that way. People are people. Fining members for every minute they're late, discouraging snack eating during the meeting—these things may work somewhere, but not on any planet we know of.

This, however, is not meant to encourage anarchy. After all, how many times have we already said that your club has to be set up and run as a business, with the social aspects a necessary and important side element?

NAIC studies confirm that clubs holding well-run, organized meetings consistently enjoy superior investment results. If you'd like to see for yourself, sit in on a model club meeting held by your local chapter. You should also become familiar with the NAIC video, "How to Run an Effective Investment Club Meeting," which is distributed to every new member club.

Organization begins with the meeting agenda. It should be e-mailed or faxed to each member prior to the meeting, along with an official invitation and the minutes of the previous meeting. This allows members to hit the ground running when the meeting begins. It also ensures that the meeting will be run according to a plan, and instills in each member a sense of professionalism akin to what they find in their job.

Please see Figure 4-09 for a sample meeting agenda, Figure 4-10 for a sample invitation and Figure 4-11 for sample minutes. Customize each for the style of your club.

The meeting itself should run as long as necessary to thoroughly cover all essential business. Two hours is typical.

You're saying be businesslike but be sociable. Can this really be done?

Absolutely, if you take it in that order. Speaking of order, the president sets the tone by beginning the meeting on time. Latecomers should get the message. After welcoming members, collecting dues and contribution checks, we recommend distributing hard copies of materials to be used in the meeting. Following that, the meeting is called to order.

The president will make any announcements ("housekeeping"), read the agenda and turn the floor over to the club secretary. After that, you're off and running.

Seems simple enough.

It really is. Even so, after 53 years of doing this, you get a sense of what works and what doesn't. Not to mention the great ideas submitted by the groups themselves. With that in mind, we proudly present...

FIGURE 4-08: 20 TIPS FOR A MORE SUCCESSFUL MEETING—PAGE 1 OF 2

1. Be flexible in setting meeting times. If it can't *always* be the fourth Wednesday of the month, then it can't. For example, Christmas might fall on that day. However, make sure that the exception is the exception.

2. Set a meeting schedule one year in advance and distribute it at your annual meeting. And don't be shy about reminding members as many times and in as many ways as necessary: phone, fax, email, a rock with a note tied to it, whatever it takes.

3. Choose a meeting location that's easy to locate. Distribute a map ahead of time. A restaurant that only you know about but others are expected to find on a cold, dark winter's night is not the way to begin the meeting.

4. Your meeting location should also be conducive to conducting business. The back room of a bar that just fixed its old mechanical bull may not be it.

5. Club officers have extra responsibilities. This may entail extra meetings for top brass prior to regular meetings. It will be worth it.

6. If your meetings regularly run into the next day, you're doing something wrong. Diagnose the problem and implement ways to streamline the session. See the next tip.

7. Consider using *Robert's Rules of Order*. You needn't run the meeting like a Senate hearing, but it shouldn't be a slumber party, either. The club president must preside. That's part of the title and that's part of the job.

8. All members need to speak up and help out. If their presentation—or any new business for which they're responsible—is due for the next meeting, they need to confirm that it will be on the meeting's agenda.

9. Proxy voting is a significant issue. On one hand, it can assure a quorum so that voting can be accomplished. Of greater concern is the crutch that it becomes for habitual absentees. Some clubs swear by it; others swear because of it.

10. *Secretaries:* don't read the minutes. Get them to the members beforehand and simply call for their approval. Most people dread speaking in public. Knowing that they're not expected to be a CNN anchorperson will make it easier to recruit the next secretary.

11. For the same reason, your club might consider having stock presentations made by teams of two rather than single members, at least for their first attempt. As long as it doesn't come out like an excerpt from "Who's on First."

12. "It's not personal, Sonny. It's strictly business," Michael Corleone said to his brother just before knocking off those two guys in the Italian restaurant. Not that you should run your club like "The Godfather," but there will be inevitable disagreements between friends about how to handle the pool of cash. Keep it cool, stick to NAIC's four principles and have someone else start your car.

13. You might also consider secret ballots on important or especially heated issues. It might save someone's life...or car.

14. Regarding visual aids: we love 'em. If you've got a presentation to make, go to the nearest copy place and have your SSG and supporting documents blown up to poster size. Your club should

FIGURE 4-08: 20 TIPS FOR A MORE SUCCESSFUL MEETING—PAGE 2 OF 2

purchase a low-cost easel for this purpose. One caution: although you should make 8 x 11 copies for everyone as handouts, hold onto them until after your presentation. Otherwise, your audience will race ahead of your speech, furiously turning pages and scanning for the information they feel is most pertinent and, as a result, taking control out of your hands. A good presenter steers the audience, not the other way around.

15. The membership of your club will probably be a great source of educational information and potential guest speakers. Poll everyone from time to time to see if anyone's second cousin of an ex-husband's army buddy once worked in the mailroom of Merck. Or something like that.

16. Hold an annual meeting in addition to monthly meetings. Its purpose will be mostly celebratory— you will have earned it—but you can also use the event to summarize and wrap up the year's progress, and perhaps even hold your elections. NAIC suggests that your club consider holding the annual meeting/elections in late March or April, so that the new treasurer can come in fresh after the club's tax returns have already been prepared.

17. Have a procedure in place to accept guest observers to your meeting. Look into other clubs' policies regarding the number of meetings a potential member must attend before declaring their candidacy for membership or being accepted as a member. You should also maintain a waiting list in the event of someone leaving the club.

18. No club is an island. Invite officers of another NAIC-affiliated club in your area to attend one of your meetings. Have them observe, take notes, and then ask them to compare your methods with theirs. You're sure to pick up a tip or two. To reciprocate, send your own delegates to their next meeting. Who knows, this could be the beginning of a beautiful friendship.

19. One of the biggest points of contention is the agonizing issue of when to eat. That depends, of course, on the time of the meeting. Sessions scheduled around breakfast or lunch are a non-issue. It's those pesky evening meetings, particularly at a member's home, that raise a red flag. The Meade Theory suggests that you "enjoy a potluck meal forty-five minutes before the meeting starts...to know (the) members better."[7] The Brown System, on the other hand, says to save supper for later. "Eating when you first arrive," she maintains, "may leave everyone sapped before the important work begins."[8] Don't look for us to be the referee; this particular food fight has left us too hungry to take sides.

20. Perhaps the most meaningful suggestion—and it's more of a critical concept—is to be consistent. Don't let potential members sitting in on one meeting leave with the impression that the next meeting may look totally different. Note that this does not fly in the face of adapting and revising your operating procedures. A consistency of purpose and investing philosophy—the very backbone of NAIC—will more than allow for some leeway as to whether the members eat before or after the meeting.

As always, these tips for more successful meetings should be merged into the style of your club. Every club is different because the people in them are different. Whatever works— that's the bottom line.

In the next chapter you'll learn how to keep the level of enthusiasm up, especially when the market is down.

INVESTMENT CLUB MONTHLY MEETING AGENDA

Welcome members

Collect membership dues/contribution checks

Distribute Club Valuation Statements

Distribute Stock Study Reports, Copies of SSG and other materials

President Calls Meeting to Order
        Announcements

Club Secretary Report
        Review and approve past meeting minutes
        Record current meeting minutes

Vice President Report
        Education program updates, needs, questions

Treasurer Report
        Update on current club financial information

Review current account/portfolio date totals (include dues collected today)
        Update on brokerage account and checking account

Reports from Computer, Education and NAIC Contacts (if applicable)

Stock to Study Reports
        Presentation of new stock studies by club members
        Review or discussion of past stock study presentations
        Update and review of stocks in portfolio

Club Member Voting Process
        Club member motions on stock study presentations accepted
        Vote on new stock study presentations for investment
        Vote on investment of current club funds

Education Program (run by the vice-president)
        Review questions from past lessons
        Conduct educational lesson plan
        Assign homework
        Review local seminars or workshop opportunities

Old Business
        Review any club business, questions or information

New Business
        NAIC communication and information
        Future needs or ideas of club; visitors scheduled, field trips, club needs

Assignments
        Stocks to study, educational program homework

Adjournment
        Announce time/date/place of next meeting

Club Social Time!

FIGURE 4-09: INVESTMENT CLUB MONTHLY MEETING AGENDA

SAMPLE OF INVITATION LETTER TO INVESTMENT CLUB MONTHLY MEETING

The Wildcat Investment Club

Dear Members:

Our regular monthly meeting will be held at 7 p.m. on **Wednesday November 10, 200x in the Baldwin Library Community Meeting Room.** The meeting should last no more than 2 hours.

The Agenda will be:

1. **Call to Order**
2. **Reading of Minutes of last meeting**
3. **Treasurer's Report**
4. **Status Reports of Current Stock Holdings:**
   a. James   – Intel Corp.
   b. Betty   – McDonald's
   c. Mary Ann – Harley Davidson
   d. Bill   – Pfizer
   e. Chris   – Home Depot
   f. Susan   – Pepsico
   g. Ken   – Synovus
5. **Presentations of 3 new stocks to consider using SSG format report**
6. **Educational session: A discussion of P/E ratios and growth rates**
7. **Old Business**
8. **New Business**
9. **Adjournment**
10. **Refreshments**

Please plan to attend! RSVP (regrets only) to the Club Secretary (email or phone call).

Next meeting: Wednesday, December 8, 200x. Bring a Guest!

FIGURE 4-10: SAMPLE INVITATION TO REGULAR MONTHLY CLUB MEETING

81

SAMPLE MINUTES OF
THE WILDCAT INVESTMENT CLUB MEETING
JANUARY 7, 200X – 7 p.m.

Present		Absent
Gary	Bruno	Leif
James	Mary Ann	Kristin
Bill	Ken	Jon
Susan	Bob	
Kim	Debra	
Mary	Michelle	

1. The meeting was called to order by president Susan.
2. The Minutes from the last meeting were read by Secretary Kim.
   a. A motion was made by Bob to accept the minutes as read.
   b. Motion seconded by Bill.
   c. Motion was approved.
3. The Financial Report was given by Ken. The net market value of the club's stocks as Dec. 31, 200x was $36,618.00. We have $1,250 in our money market account. Total assets are $37,868.00.
   a. A motion was made by Debra to accept the Financial Report.
   b. Motion was seconded by Mary.
   c. Motion was approved.
4. Stock holding updates
   a. Update reports, using SSG's, were given by James, Betty, Mary Ann, Bill, Chris, Susan, and Ken on the various stocks that they follow. A discussion followed each report.
5. New investment
   After discussing 3 potential stock purchases (presented using SSG's by James), Gary moved to purchase 50 shares of XYZ Company. Bruno seconded the motion. The motion passed.
6. Education chair, Michelle, gave a 30 minutes presentation on the topic of the night: how to read the Value Line reports.
7. The meeting was adjourned at 8:45 p.m.: motion made by Mary, seconded by Bob. Motion was approved.

The February meeting will be held on February 10th at the Baldwin Library.

FIGURE 4-11: SAMPLE OF CLUB MEETING MINUTES

Summary

Choose which type of legal entity is best for your club. Most clubs are general partnerships. If you want to invest IRA funds, you should form a limited partnership.

Once you've selected the most appropriate business entity, you have to properly register the club with federal, state and local offices.

The partnership agreement is the founding blueprint that lays out the club's general purpose, objectives and specifications. The operating procedures are the guidelines that describe the club's everyday rules and regulations.

Ask your NAIC Chapter for examples of operating procedures from other clubs. Consider your own document a work-in-progress to be refined and customized for your club.

To apply for an Employer Identification Number (a.k.a. Taxpayer Identification Number), obtain and fill out IRS Form SS-4.

Your club has to be set up and run as a business, with the social aspects a necessary and important side element. NAIC studies confirm that clubs holding well run, organized meetings consistently enjoy superior investment results.

Prior to the next meeting, the meeting agenda should be e-mailed or faxed to each member along with the minutes of the previous meeting and, of course, the time, date and location of the next meeting!

The meeting agenda and minutes should be customized for the characteristics of your club.

Use "20 Tips to a More Successful Meeting" to improve every element of your meetings.

Chapter Notes

[1] Carolyn M. Brown, *The Millionaires' Club: How to Start and Run Your Own Investment Club–and Make Your Money Grow!* (New York: John Wiley & Sons, Inc., 2000) 53-54.

[2] The NAIC sample Partnership Agreement can be downloaded from the NAIC Web Site (www.better-investing.org).

[3] The Partnership Agreement Commentary can be downloaded from the NAIC Web Site (www.better-investing.org).

[4] The NAIC sample Limited Partnership Agreement can be downloaded from the NAIC Web Site (www.better-investing.org).

[5] Ilene Meade, "How to Start an Investment Club," NAIC Investor's School, 27 Aug. 2001.

[6] Kathryn Shaw, *Investment Clubs: A Team Approach to the Stock Market* (Chicago: Dearborn Financial Publishing, Inc., 1995) 30

[7] Meade.

[8] Brown 89.

The Club Experience

In the 1972 movie "The Candidate," young and idealistic Robert Redford wins his state's Senate seat from the crusty, conservative incumbent. As he enters the hotel elevator to go down to where his screaming supporters wait, he stares blankly and mutters as the door closes, "What do I do now?"

You can't be blamed for feeling (if not looking) like Robert Redford. You've helped take a group of individuals and made them into a single unit. You've gone down to where they keep track of such things, peered across a counter and asked to be given an SS-4, and maybe felt a little like you'd have to submit to an intelligence test and several injections before they let you out of the building.

It's a daunting task, but you've done it.

OK. So now what do I do?

You do just what hundreds of thousands of club members in tens of thousands of investment clubs have done before you; you learn, you profit and you have fun. And you're ready to start now!

The Role of Club Members & Officers

Whether you call each other "members" or "partners," you are each a part of the whole. And you know what happens when one part of anything doesn't work: the entire mechanism grinds to a halt.

In your club's operating procedures, the duties of members were probably described to some extent. Note that although the three examples shown in Figures 4-5, 4-6 and 4-7 differ on many other issues, they each set down clearly what is expected of officers (and, in the latter case, the partners themselves).

Let's review (using Figure 5-01), the roles, requirements and responsibilities you will be assuming once your name is on the partnership agreement.

CLUB MEMBER ROLES, REQUIREMENTS AND RESPONSIBILITIES

Club Officers Include:
- President (Presiding Partner)
- Vice President (Assistant Presiding Partner)
- Treasurer (Financial Partner)
- Secretary (Recording Partner)
- Computer Contact
- Educational Contact
- NAIC Contact

Officers elected for one or two years. Rotate officers for learning and variety.

President's Duties:
- Set tone, pace and direction
- Demonstrate leadership skills
- Empower group to make decisions
- Motivate other members to help the club
- Write agenda for each meeting
- Encourage learning/discussions/education
- Make committee assignments
- Work with other officers to ensure the club's success
- Act as second authorized signer of checks
- Ensure that club functions according to partnership agreement and operating procedures

Vice President's Duties:
- Develop and lead educational program
- Preside in president's absence
- Purchase NAIC materials
- Invite chapter directors for club visits
- Work with officers to help develop the club
- Ensure that club members rotate education program and/or presentations
- Invite others to speak at club meetings

Treasurer's Duties:
- Transact all buy and sell orders
- Prepare monthly valuation and member status reports
- Keep records of club's financial information:
  - Investments
  - Portfolio/Stock data
  - Dividends
  - Club dues
  - Monthly deposits
  - Brokerage and bank accounts
  - Tax returns (IRS Form 1065 and Schedule K-1)
- Sign checks/reconcile bank statements
- File tax returns and assist with yearly audit
- Pay expenses incurred by club
- Consider designating an assistant treasurer to help and learn the job:
  - Treasurer receives statements/conducts record-keeping and reporting
  - Assistant treasurer collects money, makes deposits and handles disbursements

FIGURE 5-01: CLUB MEMBER ROLES, REQUIREMENTS AND RESPONSIBILITIES—PAGE 1 OF 2

Secretary's Duties:

- Record meeting minutes and distribute to members
- Record all votes, stock buy and sell orders
- Record legal and brokerage business for file copies
- Handle all correspondence
- Notify members in advance of meeting; send minutes/agenda
- Keep records of club information:
  - Maintain attendance record
  - Maintain list of club names/addresses/phone/e-mail
  - Maintain club file including Partnership Agreement, Operating Procedures, Club Archives, Member Valuations, most recent studies (including SSG) on all stocks owned and on club watch list, IRS Forms SS-4 and 1065 and Schedule K1, State/County records, other accounting records

Computer Contact Duties:

- Set up club portfolio
- Notify members of new resources on the NAIC Web Site
- Attend NAIC Chapter Computer Group meetings
- Conduct ongoing research using Internet and software

Education Contact Duties:

- Ensure that club has appropriate NAIC materials and tools
- Ensure that education program is ongoing and lively:
  - Ensure that each member receives detailed training and instruction on how to understand and use the NAIC Stock Selection Guide (SSG). This is the main tool that will allow club members to analyze a stock to make informed investment decisions. Members will learn how to complete and present a finished SSG to the club. New members can be trained by seasoned and experienced club members, use NAIC tools (software, books, videos) to self-learn the SSG and attend seminars presented by NAIC Chapters
- Plan club trips, youth education programs, other activities

NAIC Contact Duties:

- Receive and relay all communications from NAIC, including:
  - Welcome package
  - Quarterly S&P reports
  - Annual Fidelity bond
  - NAIC renewal notices
  - Chapter program notices and information

Member Duties:

- Attend meetings regularly; notify host or proper officer if unable to attend
- Learn the Stock Selection Guide and other NAIC tools
- Take a turn presenting SSG for stock purchase consideration
- Be a willing Stock Watcher and report on companies
- Pay club dues promptly
- Be willing to host a meeting
- Be willing to invite guests for membership consideration
- Complete homework and assignments in a timely manner
- Help with the annual audit
- Be willing to train for and take a turn as an officer

FIGURE 5-01: CLUB MEMBER ROLES, REQUIREMENTS AND RESPONSIBILITIES—PAGE 2 OF 2

At this juncture, we think you'll enjoy two excerpts from articles that originally appeared in NAIC's *Better Investing* magazine. They will give you vast insight into the positions of treasurer and educational chairperson.

FIGURE 5-02: CLUB MEMBERS CAN HELP THEIR TREASURER
BY AMY RAUCH-NEILSON

Rich Beaubien has been an NAIC member since the late 1980s, and one of the charter members of the NAIC Massachusetts Chapter Computer Group. Past president of the Massachusetts chapter of the NAIC and a former associate director of the Computer Group, he is currently a member of the Coast-to-Coast Online Investment Club and an adviser to the NAIC Massachusetts Chapter. He is also the former vice president of marketing for ICLUBcentral, Inc., the company that produces the *NAIC Club Accounting Software*.

Q What is the role of the club treasurer and why is it important for the club's members to understand it?

A Most club members don't understand the treasurer's job, but they need to. It's important for them to know their percentage of ownership in the club, whether their deposits have been recorded correctly and the current value of the ownership. To know those things, club members have to understand how to get there.

It's important for club members to understand the treasurer's position not only for their own sake, but also for the overall well-being of the club. Three club members who are not associated with the treasurer's position should audit a club's books every year.

Q What's the best way to educate club members about the treasurer's responsibilities?

A One of the best ways to rotate members in and out of the treasurer's job is to make it a two-year position that includes an assistant treasurer. The assistant treasurer moves into the treasurer's position at the end of the first year. That way the treasurer is always training his or her replacement. The assistant treasurer should also take classes through the local NAIC Chapter during that year of training.

Q What can club members do to make the treasurer's job easier?

A One of the ways a club can support the treasurer and make the job easier is by creating guidelines and sticking to them. In [one of the clubs I belonged to] we would meet on a Wednesday night, and the checks had to be submitted to the treasurer by Noon Saturday. The treasurer would make the deposit on the same day every month, which made the job a lot easier. Then the treasurer is free to participate in other aspects of the club, such as finding stocks and doing Stock Selection Guides.[1]

FIGURE 5-03: ESTABLISH A LONG-TERM EDUCATION STRATEGY
BY AMY RAUCH-NEILSON

Interview between Lynn Ostrem, investment club education chair, and Amy Rauch-Neilson.

Q Why is it so hard to get members to volunteer for the education chair?

A The biggest problems most clubs complain about are a lack of participation and boredom. It's my contention that a good education program will solve both problems. But most club members recoil in horror at the very thought of having to take over the education program. They perceive it to be a demanding and time-consuming task that they are not qualified to perform.

Q So how does a new education partner get started?

A Easy. There's no need to isolate yourself. There's plenty of help and material available through NAIC and the Internet. Join the I-Club-List and ask for ideas and advice. There are plenty of experienced people willing to work with you. Also, register on the NAIC CompuServe Forum. Off the Internet, you can attend NAIC classes. Most often these members are also education partners trying to pick up more knowledge.

Try to build a network of people you meet through these avenues. Some of the best writers of educational materials are club members—share that information. NAIC is all about education; it's a chain reaction.

Q What about education topics? Where do you find them?

A The NAIC Web Site is the first place to look. But topics can be found everywhere. Ask your fellow members. They know in which areas they're weak and they're a good source of ideas.

I'd also recommend the transcripts from past workshops and investor school chats. These are indispensable. So is the monthly BI Stock to Study feature. The other BI features can provide good ideas for the education segment, as well. And there are many Web sites that provide investment education. [NOTE: see the article in the March 2002 issue of *Better Investing* for a complete list of Lynn's favorite Web sites.]

Q How do you organize the subject you're going to teach? And how long should the educational segment of a club meeting last?

A I pick an idea or topic, prepare the material, and then put the five points I want to make into a 30-minute presentation. Then I e-mail the presentation to each member afterward. The second hour (of our two-hour meeting) is devoted to education. Not feeling rushed is the key. The members need to have the opportunity to ask questions.

Q Is there any parting advice you'd like to offer?

A Keep every program short and simple. Everybody learns more when they are served small, digestible pieces of information. Also, spend a few weeks planning a long-term education strategy. The program will flow better from month to month, and it will reduce the stress of having to come up with last-minute ideas.[1]

The First Year of the Club

Up until now, we've been concentrating on starting your club correctly. We've used the metaphor of an airplane to symbolize the preparation and the sequence of steps that it takes to get your club off the ground.

Continuing in this same vein, but changing the metaphor, the next two sections will deal with the rough waters out there that can cause your club to capsize. In other words, you've launched the ship; now let's make sure it's seaworthy. And if not, let's plug the leaks now before you take on too much water.

Forgive me, but any more metaphors and you can just let me go down for the third time.

We get the message. Anyway, in the first year, the energy of the members is high as they research stocks, review their (hopefully, but not always) growing portfolio and engage in lively debate. Careful organization and consistent execution remain important considerations to ensure a successful experience. Selecting members, distributing responsibilities and beginning the educational program are key elements to maintaining the terrific start that you worked hard to achieve.

So before looking too far ahead, it may be best to revisit the Ten Steps to Start Your Club, checking off what you've done and what still needs your attention:

- Hold an initial meeting.

- Find members.

- Elect officers.

- Research the partnership agreement.

- Draft operating procedures.

- Register the club with local, state and federal agencies.

- Open bank and brokerage accounts.

- Join NAIC.

- Start monthly meetings and educational programs.

- Use NAIC resources.

Many of the items above you will have had to complete before legally starting the club or buying securities. The final three are things to do as soon as possible after your inaugural meeting.

Toward the end of Year One, you'll want to take stock (so to speak) of how the club and its members are doing. Remember one of our first caveats: investment clubs are not get-rich-quick schemes, and many clubs experience small gains or even losses in the first year or longer as they acquire the kind of investing savvy that will reward them significantly over the long term.

Kathryn Shaw of Traverse City, Michigan's Women's Investment Club advises such a review every year, during which time you discuss club accomplishments and failures. As in most things, you'll usually learn more from fixing your failures than from admiring your accomplishments. Ms. Shaw also recommends starting the following year with the appointment of a steering committee. This committee of three or four members would be charged with mapping out the year ahead, developing lists of interests to explore, speakers to contact and industries to investigate.[3]

With that, your club should be well positioned to move into its second year, during which you'll be more challenged than ever to keep your ship afloat.

The Second Year & Beyond

By now, your club will have had numerous monthly meetings, completed and maybe even revised its partnership agreement and operating procedures, and made several stock transactions. Your club is settling into a routine. That's probably the biggest mistake you can make.

Whoa. Then what was all that about "careful organization and consistent execution" in the last section? Seems to me that's exactly what we've done.

True. But what you've also done is become complacent. Remember what Lynn Ostrem had to say in the article above about the club's educational program: "The biggest problems most clubs complain about are a lack of participation and boredom."

NAIC's Tom O'Hara and Kenneth Janke, Sr. tell us that keeping members interested may be the most challenging part of forming a club—perhaps even more difficult than earning a profit from your investments.

"At the outset," they remind us, "everyone is filled with enthusiasm. However, over time, particularly in a declining market, members' interests may flag. If you allow [this to happen] the potential to achieve long-term gains will vanish.

In contrast, if club members can be persuaded to continue even during long down periods, you are virtually certain to purchase stocks at bargain prices and profit handsomely when prices move upward again."[4]

That makes sense. But I'll take it a step further. We should always be thinking of keeping interest up. I'd say that an equal amount of complacency might happen when the market is riding high like in the late-1990s, when no matter what you threw your dart at you made money. Not that I get bored counting profits, but where's the real learning in that?

You know what? That really makes sense. As we said just above in reference to Ms. Shaw's year-end review suggestion, you may, indeed, learn more from failure than from success.

In order to increase and maintain interest properly, you should ideally involve all members. After you get to know everyone, you will find that different people are best suited for organizing different kinds of activities. The quietest person in the room may come up with the most memorable event, one that may even get you into *Better Investing* to share with tens of thousands of other clubs.

To get you thinking, please read the feature "10 Great Ideas to Keep Your Club On Track and Prospering." It presents some wonderful concepts to energize your club and keep members coming back.

1. Liven Up the Club Educational Program

Ask members to clip and copy relevant newspaper articles for other members. Check the Internet regularly for new information about investing. Urge members to be aware of breaking news about new company products or services. Ask members to provide an industry update related to each stock presented to or held by the club. Select a member to gather information about youth investment education and to encourage their family members to start lifetime investment programs. Provide information about NAIC's mutual fund program to club members. Many club members also own mutual funds in their individual accounts. A good educational program that continues to be developed and encouraged will help ensure your club's success.

2. Change the Meeting Atmosphere

How about holding a club meeting someplace else? Book a room at the local library, church or social hall; call a nearby restaurant with a private dining/conference area. If that's where you always meet because you think a home is too casual, try a member's family room just once; you may like it. Or, get out of the house entirely—meet at the park in the summertime. A change in environment will provide a fresh outlook.

3. Invite a Speaker to Club Meetings

Get someone from the community to liven things up with a presentation. Your local NAIC Chapter may have volunteers available to share methods of running meetings, managing portfolios or deciding on social outings. Give them a call and find out.

4. Take Field Trips

Once or twice a year, take the club on a field trip. This can be an outing related to investing, such as a visit to a local brokerage office or even the city library. Consider a visit to a local stock exchange or company headquarters if one is in your area. The outing can also be a fun day, like going to a new shopping mall or a special event in town. Some clubs go all out and celebrate their club's investment success by enjoying a cruise or other getaway with spouses and families.

5. Delegate, Delegate, Delegate

Don't allow your club to get caught in the 20-80 trap, with 20 percent of the members doing 80 percent of the work. Find out about the special talents of each member and delegate tasks to them for which they are specially suited. Create special committees to distribute the workload. Committees may include: educational development, Internet/online research, current portfolio tracking, industry updates, past stocks presented, social committee and even a snacks committee. Let the committee be creative.

6. Hold a Special Club Dinner to Socialize

Plan a special club dinner to include spouses or entire families. Consider a dinner around the holidays at a favorite local restaurant or a picnic at the park. The social aspect of your club is important, and such events provide opportunities to meet and network with members' families.

7. Stage a Debate

A debate offers the chance for club members to voice their views for or against stocks that are presented to the club. The club does not purchase some of the stocks presented. Thus, a debate allows members to make arguments for a stock, offer rebuttals and allow the group to vote for the more persuasive presentation. This provides a great way to hash out the details and aspects of a potential good or bad investment.

8. Develop a Mock Portfolio

What happens to all the stocks that are presented by club members but are not purchased by the club? Consider creating a mock portfolio and a committee to track the progress of these stocks. Your club may even decide to add one or more of them at a later date.

9. Hold a Stock-Picking Contest

Investors like to pick winners. Set some criteria for a contest so participants don't simply select the high-flying flavor of the month. One of these criteria should be NAIC's philosophy of long-term investing. For example, you may ask members to select a diverse portfolio of 15 stocks from at least eight different industries, and select a club member to report each month on the member out in front. The winner will, of course, receive a nice prize. Contests and games add some fun to the educational aspect of investment clubbing.

10. Teach Others in Your Community about Investing

Many people join an investment club to learn about investing. Consider your club as a teaching tool. Club members should visit a local school to teach young people about investing and investment clubs. Visit a local service organization or church to stage a mock club meeting. Helping others to learn about investing is, after all, the very mission of NAIC. Your club can help. There's a funny thing that many NAIC employees and volunteers have experienced. The more we reach out to help others, it seems the more we get back in return.[5]

Great ideas there, Mr. Strong. I especially like the suggestion about contests. How about making up our own version of a TV game show with questions or challenges about investing?

Excellent. You're in charge. Actually, great ideas come from members all over the country as well as from our other credited sources. Here, then, are some additional ways to

make your club experience fun as well as profitable. Some are expanded or offshoot versions of those on Jonathan's list, and some are wonderfully original.

More Field Trips

In addition to the library, a brokerage, the stock exchange and a local company's headquarters, plan to attend at least one corporate annual meeting of a stock your club owns or is considering, if that's possible in your area. It's a true learning experience. If there isn't a company headquarters within traveling distance, visit a branch or other representation of the

company or product. They're usually willing to give some personal attention to a group of shareholders.

The Women of Wealth (WOW) of Bossier City, Louisiana have held dinner meetings at Wendy's, one of its major holdings. Financial partner Pat Berry reports, "We visited a rig site where Nabors Industries [in which they also own stock] was drilling a gas well. Now *that* was an enlightening—

and hot—experience."[6] The ladies also own a bit of Harley-Davidson, and we can only imagine the minutes of that meeting.

More Contests

Jonathan Strong's stock-picking contest invites a number of variations on the theme. Your members can guess where the DJIA or the NASDAQ will be six months or a year in the future. Or, they can take a stab at how much one stock in the club's portfolio—or the entire portfolio, for that matter—will be worth at a certain time down the road.

If you're the quizmaster, try and work in as many questions as you can about the club's own holdings, such as the last reported dividend, yield or P/E.

FIGURE 5-04: WOMEN OF WEALTH INVESTMENT CLUB

More Prizes

How about naming your own MVP—Most Valuable Partner? Give out an award at your annual meeting to acknowledge the member who's done the most during the year to further the club's goals. It might seem obvious to pick the president or treasurer, but you'll find that important and lasting contributions can come from virtually anyone.

More Reaching Out

Once you've been on the receiving end of help from other clubs in your area and you're far enough along, it's time to give back. Make yourselves available to mentor the new investors on the block. Tell your NAIC Chapter that there are members in your club who are available to go to a meeting of a fledgling club and hold their hands through the start-up process.

You won't have to pay taxes on the dividends you'll receive from investing in your community. Volunteer time to do some good for your neighbors. You know best what will work. The Women in Black of Sammamish, Washington complete a charitable project

FIGURE 5-05: WOMEN IN BLACK INVESTMENT CLUB

each year. Most recently, they collected toiletry items and assembled 100 "Mother's Day bags" to donate for distribution through a local charity.[7]

More Education

Tap the member who knows computers and can spell, too, to put together a club newsletter. A quarterly should be more than sufficient. You can even publish your own annual report, including a year-end valuation statement.

More Parties

Can't get enough of each other? Don't wait for a holiday to party hearty.

You might, for instance, use the outstanding long-term performance of one of your holdings as an excuse. And don't forget the other NAIC-affiliated clubs in your area. By pooling your party funds with theirs, you can afford together what you couldn't individually. Which is, after all, one of the reasons you're in an investment club to begin with.

Summary

Whether you call each other "members" or "partners," you are each a part of the whole.

Club officers include: President (Presiding Partner), Vice President (Assistant Presiding Partner), Treasurer (Financial Partner), Secretary (Recording Partner), Computer Contact, Educational Contact and NAIC Contact. Officers are elected for one or two years. Rotate officers for learning and variety.

Member Duties:

- Attend meetings regularly; notify host or proper officer if unable to attend
- Learn the Stock Selection Guide and other NAIC tools
- Take a turn presenting SSG for stock purchase consideration
- Be a willing Stock Watcher and report on companies
- Pay club dues promptly
- Be willing to host a meeting
- Be willing to invite guests for membership consideration
- Complete homework and assignments in a timely manner
- Help with the annual audit
- Be willing to train for and take a turn as an officer

In the first year, the energy of the members is high as they research stocks, review their (hopefully, but not always) growing portfolio and engage in lively debate. Careful organization and consistent execution remain important considerations to ensure a successful experience. Education is also of prime importance; the second part of this book is designed to help make it enjoyable as well as a learning adventure.

Conduct a year-end review every year, during which time you discuss club accomplishments and failures. You'll usually learn more from fixing your failures than from admiring your accomplishments. Start the following year with the appointment of a Steering Committee, charged with mapping out the year ahead.

Keeping members interested may be the most challenging part of forming a club—perhaps even more difficult than earning a profit from your investments. At the outset, everyone is filled with enthusiasm. However, over time, particularly in a declining market, members' interests may flag. If club members can be persuaded to continue even during long down periods, you are virtually certain to purchase stocks at bargain prices and profit handsomely when prices move upward again.

In order to increase and maintain interest properly, you should ideally involve all members. After you get to know everyone, you will find that different people are best suited for organizing different kinds of activities. The quietest person in the room may come up with the most memorable event.

"10 Great Ideas to Keep Your Club on Track and Prospering" include: liven up the club educational program; change the meeting atmosphere; invite a speaker to club meetings; take field trips; delegate; hold a special club dinner to socialize; stage a debate; develop a second mock portfolio; hold a stock-picking contest; and teach others in your community about investing.

Chapter Notes

[1] Rauch-Neilson, "Club Members Can Help Their Treasurer," *Better Investing* February 2002: 34-35.

[2] Amy Rauch-Neilson, "Establish a Long-term Education Strategy," *Better Investing* March 2002: 32-33, 39.

[3] Kathryn Shaw, *Investment Clubs: A Team Approach to the Stock Market* (Chicago: Dearborn Financial Publishing, Inc., 1995) 99,103.

[4] Thomas E. O'Hara and Kenneth S. Janke, Sr., *Starting and Running a Profitable Investment Club* (New York: Times Books, 1998) 197.

[5] Jonathan Strong, "10 Great Ideas to Keep Your Club on Track and Prospering."

[6] "Real-life Stories from Clubs and Individuals," *Better Investing* November 2001: 8.

[7] "Real-life Stories...": 8.

Investment Club Accounting

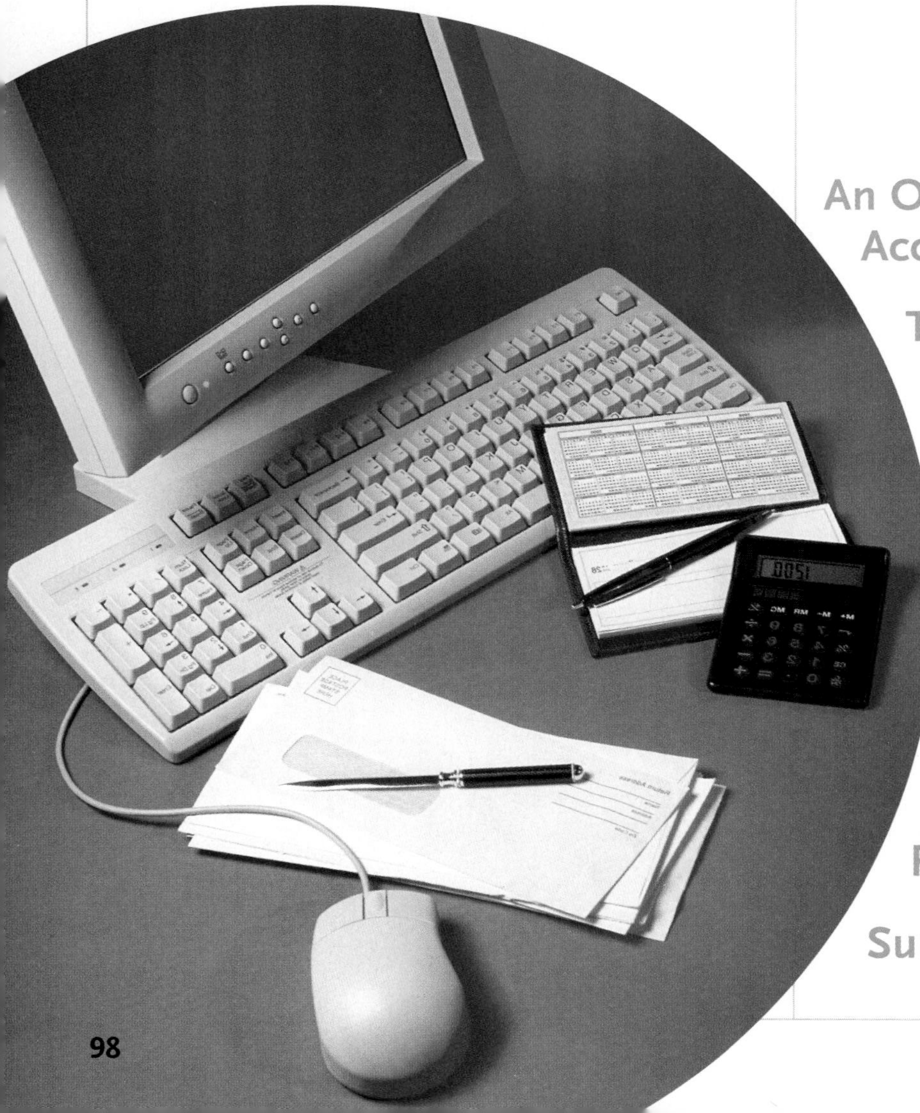

An Overview of NAIC Club Accounting Methods

The Valuation Unit System

The Valuation Statement

Membership Changes: Full and Partial Withdrawals, New Members

Online Accounting Resources

Tax Information and Resources/Sample Forms

Summary

Chapter 5 presented many ideas to maintain member interest, from parties and games—to more parties and games. Chapter 6 will offer ways to ensure that each member's share of club funds is accurately recorded and reported, so it's all there when you want it.

First, a little background. When the first NAIC investment clubs considered their accounting needs they recognized that the membership of most clubs would not necessarily include individuals with bookkeeping credentials. Since they hoped every member would take a shot at the post of treasurer (financial partner) or assistant treasurer to broaden their investment knowledge, NAIC designed their accounting system with the inexperienced bookkeeper in mind. In fact, Tom O'Hara designed it in 1940 for the Mutual Investment Club of Detroit.

Oh great—we're using a system from when Franklin D. Roosevelt was president.

A system? In some ways, yes. The philosophies and strategies that worked then have held up amazingly well. But the tools are strictly state-of-the-art and constantly updated and upgraded.

But back to the story. The system was simplified through the years to the maximum extent consistent with good business practices, and provides all the information required by the club, its individual members and governmental agencies. It has been time-tested by thousands of clubs operating as partnerships.

As you and your club begin to keep records, remember the keyword: accuracy. NAIC has several tools to help. The *NAIC Investment Club Accounting*

Handbook can help your treasurer understand the accounting concepts pertaining to your club, as well as how to keep your books manually. Club accounting software is also available. You can download a demo of *NAIC Club Accounting Software* by visiting the NAIC Web Site— www.better-investing.org. Or use NAIC Online Club Accounting available at http://naic-club.com. The software tutorials and the "Help" key will take you through every step. And of course, NAIC customer support is just a phone call or keystroke away.[1]

An Overview of NAIC Club Accounting Methods

One of the first tasks for your newly formed club is setting up the books. You need to come up with a process to track every cash transaction and to calculate every member's share of the whole. You can accomplish this important task in four ways:

1. *By hand using the NAIC Investment Club Accounting Handbook and prepared forms.*

2. *Electronically using NAIC Club Accounting Software.*

3. *By hiring an outside bookkeeper or accountant to maintain the books for the club.*

No matter which process you choose to use, the treasurer is ultimately responsible for club record keeping. However, it is highly recommended that each member of the club become somewhat familiar with the process.

Each member should also be prepared to audit the work of the treasurer if asked to do so. The NAIC chapter nearest you offers periodic programs on record keeping and tax reporting. At the very least, the club's treasurer and members of the audit committee should attend these sessions.[2]

Investment club accounting can be divided into two positions: the treasurer and assistant treasurer. Here's one way of dividing the chores:

The **TREASURER** *maintains records of the club's financial affairs.*

1. Handles the recording of all transactions in the journal or club accounting software.

2. Prepares monthly Valuation Statements.

3. Prepares distribution reports and tax returns.

The **ASSISTANT TREASURER** *maintains records of the members' interests, or members' shares of the club's assets.*

1. Handles all funds paid into or withdrawn from the club.

2. Contacts the broker to make purchases, sales or transfers of stock.

Besides reducing the workload of the treasurer, this plan can act as an apprenticeship program, prepping the assistant treasurer to smoothly assume the duties of the treasurer following an election of club officers. Again, the *NAIC Investment Club Accounting Handbook* and *NAIC Club Accounting Software*

are designed to make all the number crunching well within the limits of the average club member.

Let's get to the good part: how do I know what my share of the club's assets is worth?

To appraise each individual member's share of ownership, we recommend the NAIC accounting system. The system uses as its basis an important term that you'll come to know and appreciate: the Valuation Unit.

The Valuation Unit System

This system is similar to the one used by mutual funds. If you're a fund investor, you know that a fund's share price is calculated by dividing net assets by shares outstanding. This is the share's Net Asset Value (NAV), and it's what you would pay for one share of that fund.

In this system of Valuation Units, your club is an investment making enterprise issuing partnership units, and selling these to a limited clientele. The value of one Valuation Unit in your club is computed the same way as the NAV—by dividing the dollar value of club assets by the number of Valuation Units issued by the club.

The formula looks like this:

$$\frac{\text{Total \$ Value of Club Assets}}{\text{Number of Valuation Units}} = \text{\$ Value of 1 Valuation Unit}$$

You still there?

So far, so good.

Excellent. The main reason that this system works so well for investment clubs is that it accommodates unequal ownership of club assets. It's nice to think that each of you will be putting in an equal amount of money every month to buy the same amount of shares in the same stocks. Realistically and over the long term, it doesn't work that way.

The Valuation Unit System permits members to increase or decrease their monthly investment or to make partial withdrawals. It also anticipates changes in membership, allowing new members to come in fresh with their minimum monthly payment, rather than having to "buy out" the interest of the departing member.

If your club is already in operation but using a different system, have your treasurer consult the *NAIC Investment Club Accounting Handbook* to learn the procedure for converting to the Valuation Unit System.

It sounds great, but how come the members don't just get equal ownership in the club? Isn't that easier and fairer?

It's been our experience that clubs endeavoring to maintain financial equality don't see the bigger picture. We already mentioned the cases in which members want to contribute dissimilar monthly amounts or new members come in and have to "put up" what everyone else has accumulated after years of small, regular contributions.

There are other examples of inequity. Members who pay late should not be equal partners. Under the Valuation Unit System, if a member pays late and the value of the club has gone up since the last meeting, that money will buy fewer units than the money invested on time.

If a member needs money for an unexpected emergency or special need, how do you accommodate a partial withdrawal and still keep that member an equal partner? You can't.

Finally, there is the matter of one-person-one-vote vs. voting based on the numbers of units owned, as with stock shareholders. To forestall any misunderstanding, your partnership agreement should specify a maximum percentage of total units that can be owned by any single member. In the operating procedures, stipulate method and basis of voting. See Figures 4-1, 4-6 and 4-7 as examples.

The Valuation Statement

The valuation of an investment club member's interest is different from valuation in other businesses.

Why is that?

Two main reasons. First, because the worth of club assets is constantly fluctuating due to stock market changes. Second, most clubs are partnerships, so each person owns part of the total assets rather than shares of stock, as in a corporation. All of the assets must be valued whenever members deposit additional funds, which is monthly in most clubs. Each member's account consists of two parts: the accumulation of cash deposits and a valuation record of his or her deposits, which includes the sum of profits and losses.[4]

Prior to each monthly meeting, a Valuation Statement is prepared by the club treasurer. In its briefest form, the Valuation Statement displays the securities owned by the club and their total current value, the amount of cash on hand, the current value of one Valuation Unit and the number of Valuation Units that can be purchased with $10.00.

How do you get the $10.00?

Good question. The Valuation Units of an investment club originate at the time the first funds are paid into the club by its members. At that first issue of Units, their value is arbitrarily set at $10.00 each. Thereafter, the value of a Unit will be more or less than $10.00, reflecting the change in share value of securities in the club's portfolio.

As a result, after its first month of operation the club will never issue a Unit for exactly $10.00. Each $10.00 will buy a fraction more or a fraction less than one Unit.

Let's look at an example. In May, 2004, John Smith, Sue Jones and Mary Brown formed ABC Investment Club. Their first meeting was held in June, 2004. At this meeting, each member contributed $120 and received twelve units each. The club voted unanimously to purchase twenty shares of XYZ Corporation. The purchase was made on June 15, 2004 for a total cost of $344.80, including fees and taxes. This amount, deducted from the $360 on deposit with the broker, leaves a cash balance of $15.20.

In short, maintaining "equality" is not necessarily fair to the more conscientious members, it has the potential to limit growth, and can even threaten the existence of a club. By using the Valuation Unit System, your club can attract and retain members without imposing a financial barrier.[3]

FIGURE 6-01: ABC INVESTMENT CLUB VALUATION STATEMENT: JULY 11, 2004

Company	# Shares	Cost/ Share	Total Cost	Price/ Share (this date)	Total Value
XYZ Corp.	20	$17.24	$344.80	$16.125	$322.50
Cash on Hand					15.20
Total Value of Club					$337.70
Total Number of Valuation Units Issued to Date					36
Value of Each Unit ($337.70 / 36 Units)					$ 9.38
Number of Units each $10.00 Will Purchase ($10.00 / $9.38)					1.0661

Figure 6-01 shows a sample Valuation Statement in its briefest form as it might look after the club's first month of operation.

The July 11 statement describes the club's financial condition at the beginning of the second meeting. At this meeting, $10.00 will purchase 1.0661 Units.

Note that the Valuation Unit decreased in value from $10.00 to $9.38 during the first month of operation of the club, reflecting the reduction in the club's asset value. You should be prepared for a similar experience. Although it may be disappointing, this is to be expected, since the costs to purchase the stock must be absorbed. Under normal marketing conditions, the price of any purchased issue would seldom increase during one month in an amount that would compensate for these costs.

New clubs will find that making purchases through NAIC's Low Cost Investment Program (covered in the next chapter) may reduce the cost of their purchases. While there is a small set up fee, additional purchases can often be made for little or no cost.

Figure 6-01 includes all the information required in a Valuation Statement. Many clubs, however, add other information deemed helpful to portfolio management, such as Dividend, P/E Ratio and Projected High/Low Price for the Next Five Years. Many clubs also combine this report with the details of member purchases and ownership of Valuation Units. The extent of this report is up to the club treasurer.[5]

Membership Changes: Full & Partial Withdrawals, New Members

Many NAIC-affiliated clubs have been around for decades, as have many of their individual members. But like car commercials that warn, "Your mileage may vary," so may your investment club.

Bear in mind, though, that members come and go for a million reasons. They move. They can't make the meetings. They have another baby. They start or join another club.

One of the beauties of the Valuation Unit System is that it easily accounts for changes in ownership of the club.

This section will cover the procedure for making payoffs to existing members, either through a "full withdrawal" or a "partial withdrawal." Following that is the process of adding a new member.

As it is the purpose of this book to educate all members in the operations of the entire club, particularly record keeping, the content level in this section, as in the previous one, will be basic.

There are obviously complex tax considerations that go hand in hand with the kinds of transactions to be discussed here. Your treasurer should therefore become familiar, to say the least, with the appropriate chapters in the *NAIC Investment Club Accounting Handbook* and the proper use of *NAIC Club Accounting software*. And you, as a member, must know what

triggers a taxable event and how the IRS treats capital gains distributions to you as both a club partner and as an individual.

As long as we're being basic, here's one basic rule for anything you'll do under this section:

Put It In Writing

Whether you're a member requesting a withdrawal or a club reporting one, there's the inevitable paperwork that comes before, during and after. Don't let it fall through the cracks. You might take a fall with it.

The Full Withdrawal

The remaining members of an investment club choose the payment option for the members making a full withdrawal. These payment options include:

- Cash
- Securities
- Combination of cash and securities

There are two ways to obtain the cash for a full withdrawal. First, the club may have enough cash on hand, or money contributed from the remaining members to pay the withdrawing member out. If this is not the case, the club may consider selling securities.

When selling securities, the club should consider factors such as whether or not the

Or, in some cases, they just plain don't like the rest of you.

Or vice versa.

That's right. And you, as a club, need to protect yourself by having provisions for any eventuality, up to and including a member's relocation, family circumstances and yes, even a personality conflict that results in a member leaving or being asked to leave.

security is overpriced or perhaps has out-performed their growth potential. A thorough study of a stock using the *NAIC Stock Selection Guide* should be made before making a decision. Figure 6-02 lists the tax implications for the departing member, the club and its remaining members. Again, this information is being presented in its most basic form and is not to be taken as tax or legal advice.

Before any withdrawal is transacted, the treasurer must do a partial closing of the books to determine the withdrawing member's portion of any

taxable items, such as expenses and dividend income. These amounts, as well as certain personal information, must be declared on the member's K-1 tax form as well as on his or her personal return.

In addition, the withdrawal itself will be treated as a sale of an investment; all capital gains will have to likewise be reported on the withdrawing member's personal return for the current year.

The Partial Withdrawal

Members are entitled to their money. Things like unexpected medical expenses or an

appliance that breaks down are just the sorts of "rainy days" that you save for in the first place. But is your investment club account the best place from which to draw cash? Think about it.

The tax implications of a partial withdrawal can be more complex than for a complete withdrawal, depending upon how the member is paid and the source of cash funds that are used. Because of these tax implications, the member making the partial withdrawal chooses whether to be paid in cash or securities (but not which securities they receive).

FIGURE 6-02: FULL WITHDRAWAL FROM AN INVESTMENT CLUB

WITHDRAWAL PAYMENT OPTION	TAX IMPLICATION
1. Withdrawing member is paid out with cash on hand.	1. Withdrawing member realizes gain/loss based on difference between cost basis in the club and cash received.
2. Club sells stock at a gain to raise cash for withdrawing member.	2. All members (including withdrawing member) realize pro-rata share of gain on stock sale.
3. Club sells stock at a loss to raise cash for withdrawing member.	3. All members (including withdrawing member) realize pro-rata share of loss on stock sale.
4. Club issues appreciated stock to withdrawing member.	4. Withdrawing member realizes no gain until he/she sells the stock. For remaining members, no current gain is realized.
5. Club issues stock held at a loss to withdrawing member.	5. Withdrawing member realizes no gain/loss until he/she sells the stock. For remaining members, no current loss is realized. **NOTE:** If the club wants to remove the stock from its portfolio, a more advantageous move is to sell the stock (so all members get a write-off) and issue cash to the withdrawing member.[6]

Your club treasurer should refer to the *NAIC Investment Club Accounting Handbook* for details. It is also recommended that IRS Publication 541—Partnerships be consulted.

Figure 6-03 lists the tax implications for the departing member, the club and its remaining members. Again, this information is being presented in its most basic form and is not to be taken as tax or legal advice.

The transfer of securities from a club's portfolio to a withdrawing member is easily accomplished. A letter signed by the club's agent (remember, the treasurer acts in this capacity) is sent to the broker. The letter specifies the number of shares of the issue to be transferred, the member's name and the effective date of transfer. The member receiving the stock must already have an individual account with this broker.[8]

FIGURE 6-03: PARTIAL WITHDRAWAL FROM AN INVESTMENT CLUB	
WITHDRAWAL PAYMENT OPTION	**TAX IMPLICATION**
1. Withdrawing member is paid out with cash on hand.	1. Withdrawing member's cost basis in the club is reduced by the amount of the withdrawal, down to, but not below, zero. If the withdrawal amount exceeds their cost basis in the club, they must treat the excess as a capital gain in the year in which the withdrawal is made.
2. Club sells stock at a gain to raise cash for withdrawing member.	2. All members (including withdrawing member) realize pro-rata share of gain on stock sale. Withdrawing member also realizes an additional gain upon withdrawal if the cash withdrawn exceeds their cost basis in the club.
3. Club sells stock at a loss to raise cash for withdrawing member.	3. All members realize pro-rata share of loss on stock sale. Withdrawing member may also realizes a gain upon withdrawal if the cash withdrawn exceeds their cost basis in the club.
4. Club issues appreciated stock to withdrawing member.	4. Withdrawing member's cost basis in the transferred stock is equal to the club's cost basis in that stock (not to exceed the withdrawing members cost basis in the club). Any gain or loss is deferred until the stock is sold.
5. Club issues stock held at a loss to withdrawing member.	5. Withdrawing member's cost basis in the transferred stock is equal to the club's cost basis in that stock. (not to exceed the withdrawing members cost basis in the club). Any gain or loss is deferred until the stock is sold.[7]

Be advised that the general provisions for a withdrawal from an individual's capital account should be firmly set in your partnership agreement.

Figure 6-04 illustrates how the Mutual Investment Club of Detroit Partnership Agreement, which serves as the model for all others, anticipates various grounds for withdrawals. On the left are the applicable paragraphs; on the right, each is interpreted.

FIGURE 6-04: HOW THE MUTUAL INVESTMENT CLUB OF DETROIT PARTNERSHIP AGREEMENT PROVIDES FOR MEMBER WITHDRAWALS—PAGE 1 OF 3

PARTNERSHIP AGREEMENT PARAGRAPH	WHAT IT MEANS
16B—Removal of Partner Any partner may be removed by agreement of the partners whose capital accounts total a majority of the value of all partners' capital accounts. Written notice of a meeting where removal of a partner is to be considered shall include a specific reference to the matter. The removal shall become effective upon payment of the value of the removed partner's capital account, which shall be in accordance with the provisions on full withdrawal of a partner noted in paragraphs 18 and 20. The vote action shall be treated as receipt of request for withdrawal.	• This provision can be used when there is someone in the club who is not doing their share of the work or is missing meetings. • It is seldom used; members usually resign of their own free will.
18—Voluntary Withdrawal Any partner may withdraw a part or all of the value of his capital account in the partnership and the partnership shall continue as a taxable entity. The partner withdrawing a portion or all of the value of his capital account shall give notice of such intention in writing to the Secretary. Written notice shall be deemed to be received as of the first meeting of the partnership at which it is presented. If written notice is received between meetings it will be treated as received at the first following meeting. In making payment, the value of the partnership as set forth in the valuation statement prepared for the first meeting following the meeting at which the written notice is received from a partner requesting a partial or full withdrawal, will be used to determine the value of the partner's capital account. The partnership shall pay the partner who is withdrawing a portion or all of the value of his capital account in the partnership in accordance with paragraph 20 of the Agreement.	• Any withdrawal request needs to be in writing and given to the secretary. • If it is brought to a meeting, it is recorded as received at that meeting. • If it is brought to the secretary between meetings, it should be brought up at the next scheduled meeting. • The withdrawing member is valued and paid out (in cash or securities) at the first meeting AFTER the meeting where the withdrawal notice is presented. • Refer to Paragraph 20 for payment instructions.

19—Death or Incapacity of a Partner

In the event of the death or incapacity of a partner (or the death or incapacity of the grantor and sole trustee of a revocable living trust, if such trust is a partner pursuant to Paragraph 16A hereof), receipt of notice of such event shall be treated as notice of full withdrawal.

- The date of their death can be used as the date of their withdrawal notice.

- Use Paragraph 20 and follow these procedures when paying the member out.

- DO NOT transfer funds (cash or stock) to someone else unless specifically ordered by the estate in writing. Consult an attorney if you have any doubts.

20—Terms of Payment

In the case of a partial withdrawal, payment may be made in cash or securities of the partnership or a mix of each at the option of the partner making the partial withdrawal.

In the case of a full withdrawal, payment may be made in cash or securities or a mix of each at the option of the remaining partners.

In either case, where securities are to be distributed, the remaining partners select the securities.

Where cash is transferred, the partnership shall transfer to the partner (or other appropriate entity) withdrawing a portion of all of his interest in the partnership, an amount equal to the lesser of (I) ninety-seven percent (97%) of the value of the capital account in the partnership being withdrawn or (ii) the value of the capital account being withdrawn, less the actual cost to the partnership of selling securities to obtain cash to meet the withdrawal. The amount being withdrawn shall be paid within 10 days after the evaluation date used in determining the withdrawal amount.

If a partner withdrawing a portion or all of the value of his capital account in the partnership desires an immediate payment in cash, the partnership at its earliest convenience may pay eighty percent (80%) of the estimated value of his capital account and settle the balance in accordance with the valuation and payment procedures set forth in paragraphs 18 and 20.

- The withdrawing partner does not get to select which securities they should receive.

- The larger of a 3% fee (3% of the amount they are to receive in cash) or transaction costs (mainly brokerage commissions) can be charged to the withdrawing partner.

- It is not recommended that clubs charge their members "penalties" for leaving.

- Sometimes a member is making a partial or full withdrawal because they are in urgent need of cash. If the club has this money available, they can pay the member 80% of their estimated worth as soon as feasibly possible.

- Transfer of securities allows the club to postpone capital gains.

- The withdrawing partner has no capital gain on the transaction until they sell the securities.

- The withdrawing partner may need to have a brokerage account to transfer securities into.

- DRP accounts can be easily set up.

FIGURE 6-04: HOW THE MUTUAL INVESTMENT CLUB OF DETROIT PARTNERSHIP AGREEMENT PROVIDES FOR MEMBER WITHDRAWALS—PAGE 3 OF 3

When securities are transferred, the partnership shall select securities to transfer equal to the value of the capital account or a portion of the capital account being withdrawn (i.e. without a reduction for broker commissions). Securities shall be transferred as of the date of the club's valuation statement prepared to determine the value of that partner's capital account in the partnership. The Club's broker shall be advised that ownership of the securities has been transferred to the partner as of the valuation date used for the withdrawal.

- Securities should be transferred the date of the valuation statement that is prepared to determine the value. This allows the member to sell the security and receive the same amount of money as they would if they received cash.

Adding New Members

If losing a member is hard—emotionally and mathematically—then bringing in a new member is as easy as getting a signature on the partnership agreement. Almost.

I would think that it's natural to want to enroll a new member right after the old member leaves, to preserve the status quo.

It is. But don't rush into things. You're not getting dentures; you don't have to fill the space.

Don't we have to replace old money with new money dollar for dollar?

Why? You have to look at your club's assets as a single investment portfolio instead of a lot of individual ones. If you sell off a stock that you hold in your personal portfolio, you don't feel the need to buy another stock of equal value, do you?

No.

Adding a new member does not "balance" the effect of the departing member. If you do bring in a new member hot on the heels of the departing one, the new member is not "buying out" the old one. The transactions are and must be kept separate. The Valuation Unit System was set up with the clear expectation that member rotation was inevitable, and therefore makes new member initiation painless to the pocketbook.

Nor does the new member have to "catch up" with the remaining members. Under the Unit System, the new member may blend right in and start making the same monthly contribution as other members. The valuation unit determined each month will relate the value of his or her holdings to those other members. Of course, a new member's value will be considerably lower than the value of long-standing members.

Member Recruitment

Adding to the rolls may only take a phone call to a neighbor or family member who's already on your club's waiting list. More typically, it takes much more. And it should—for the protection of both the club and the recruit.

We've emphasized throughout that although you call yourselves a "club," you're not a bunch of kids swapping Barbie doll accessories after school. You're putting up serious dollars and pursuing a very specific course of long-term investing that isn't for everyone. We repeat here the caution from Chapter 1:

> **It is a fact that some new investment clubs go out of business within the first twelve to eighteen months. Reasons include: inability to start a systematic education program, social difficulties and differing investment philosophies because of a conflict between those who believe in long-term investing and those who advocate speculative trading.**

Those words should hang over your head like a sign over the fireplace.

So how do we keep from being in that group that doesn't make it?

To ensure that people interested in joining have a clear understanding of the club's goals and its strategies to achieve them, most clubs have an effective screening/initiation process in place.

According to authors Gerlach and McQuade in an informative series of articles appearing in *Better Investing,* a prospective member should have a chance to review the club's partnership agreement and operating procedures. He/she should also be clear on the club's requirements for minimum meeting attendance and annual number of stock and/or educational presentations.[9]

Many clubs, they point out, have an initiation or probationary period during which candidates attend meetings and even participate. This serves as an "audition," of sorts, and it's a two-way street.

What do you mean?

Your club is "casting" for a member who will add to your club's strength and stability. As part of the casting session, you'll be testing their willingness and ability to make such a contribution. At the same time, the candidates are looking all of you over to be sure they want to spend their valuable time with you.

How can we help each other to determine if it's a good mutual fit?

Some clubs appoint a membership officer who may create a prospective member packet. Figure 6-05 gives you an idea of what to include. In addition, this person or another one will serve as a mentor to candidates, guiding them through whatever internship process the club has in place. During this probationary period, they'll learn the ropes while putting away the monthly contribution amount to ante in upon admission to the club.

FIGURE 6-05: PROSPECTIVE MEMBER PACKET

Items to Include:

- Application Form
- Club History
- Description of Club Objectives and Investment Philosophy
- Copy of the club partnership agreement and operating procedures
- List of member expectations and responsibilities
- List of current club portfolio
- Education program requirements
- Stock presentation requirements
- Sample completed Stock Selection Guide
- Software purchase requirements
- Initial and monthly contribution amounts
- Schedule of upcoming meeting dates/locations
- Contact information
- Internship program requirements

Questions to Include:

- What is your investing experience?
- Have you ever been a member of an investment club?
- Do you have time to fulfill the responsibilities of club membership?
- Can you consistently make our club's minimum monthly financial contribution?
- Are you willing to serve as a club officer at some point?
- Do you have access to a computer and the Internet?
- Are you willing to consistently perform the membership responsibilities outlined in this packet?
- Are you able to attend educational classes outside of regular monthly meetings?

Club Responsibilities

There are very few restrictions and requirements your club must observe in its pursuit of the perfect membership.

Thou Shalt Not Advertise

The line between being a harmless club and an unlicensed broker is not an exceptionally thin one. The government has better things to do than police 23,000 clubs with nearly 265,000 members. That said, there is, nevertheless, a line that you should be careful not to cross.

Putting out the word that you're looking for members—either to form a brand new club or to replace an exiting partner—is something best done by word of mouth. Posting a notice on the bulletin board at your church or workplace is inching closer to that unspecified "neutral zone," but nobody we know of has been visited by two men in trench coats flashing badges and a court order to take down the sign.

Inserting an ad in a local newspaper is tantamount to putting your toe on that line. If the content of your ad uses words like "guaranteed returns" or "it'll put your kid through medical school," you've probably just made a "public offering of a security" and someone's going to come a knockin'.

Other than word of mouth, your best bet is to contact the NAIC chapter nearest you. NAIC is bound by the same regulations as its member clubs, and therefore cannot advertise investment clubs or provide names/addresses of club or individual members. Nor can it provide names of prospective members to existing clubs or those in the planning stages. However, by attending chapter meetings and making your needs known, you'll be networking with prospective members in no time.

Revise the Partnership Agreement and Operating Procedures

As soon as the vote is in, make arrangements to add and/or delete member names to all appropriate club documents. In Chapter 4, you learned of the need to do so, especially in the case of departing members who no longer have rights in the organization. If it's a simple matter of the club bringing in someone new you might consider having the new member sign a statement endorsing the provisions of the agreement until such time as it's officially redrafted.

Notify NAIC

Club members renew as a group once a year. Changes, of course, can and should be submitted as soon as possible. Use the forms that are available on the NAIC Web Site, or simply send changes in writing. State your club name, club membership number and note the member changes along with any payment due.

Online Accounting Resources

Listed in Figure 6-06 are some handy Internet sites to find investment club accounting information, advice and links. See Chapter 10 for additional site directories.

Tax Information & Resources/Sample Forms

'Twas the night before tax time
And all through the land,
Investment club members
Could not understand.
"This money is mine,
My withdrawals were none.
So why did I receive
A Schedule K-1?"

That's terrible.

Sorry. We never said our poetry was good.

Not that. Paying taxes on money I haven't seen.

Well, you can try dumping tea in the harbor, but that's already been done. What's important is that you grasp the system and learn how to make it work best for you.

Investment clubs, like other entities, have to be aware of the tax rules that apply to them and to their members.

Our purpose here is to introduce you to the overall tax and reporting requirements you assume when you start an investment club.

FIGURE 6-06: INVESTMENT CLUB ACCOUNTING WEB SITES

WEB SITE	DESCRIPTION
www.better-investing.org	NAIC offers investors a Web site and forum that provides comprehensive information about NAIC, educational content, library files, data and information for downloading. These online resources provide the opportunity to interact with other NAIC members via the I-Club-List discussion group and the Message Area of the NAIC Forum on CompuServe. Investors and NAIC members can meet to share ideas, study stocks, receive help and advice and even ask questions or place orders with the NAIC membership services group. NAIC Online also maintains a library of helpful files, including electronic copies of some of NAIC's brochures, archives of discussions, data files that can be used with NAIC software products, and demos, spreadsheets, club partnership agreements and other valuable information.
www.naic-club.com	The site of NAIC Online Club Accounting (NOCA). Created by ICLUBcentral, this tool offers NAIC investment clubs a home on the Internet to maintain their club records in the form of a private Web site.
www.fool.com/InvestmentClub	The Motley Fool Web site area dedicated to investment clubs and members.
www.irs.gov	Download any of the tax forms discussed here.
www.wfic.org	The site of the World Federation of Investors Corp., of which NAIC is a member.
www.douglasgerlach.com/clubs	This site run by Douglas Gerlach contains much useful information specifically designed for investment club members.
www.iclub.com	A comprehensive directory of investment clubs and NAIC-related resources, including accounting tools for downloading. Douglas Gerlach is on this site, too. ICLUBcentral makes NAIC's club accounting software.
www.sec.gov	The Securities and Exchange Commission site is where to find all SEC regulations.

year, the club files an information return —Form 1065 to report each income and expense item, as well as the portion distributed to each member.'

So I don't pay taxes, then.

On the contrary: club members are personally liable for payment of their share of the club's income.

But I didn't take any out; it's just sitting there growing, only not as fast as I thought, apparently.

One concept that many people have trouble understanding is the difference between profit and withdrawal. As a partnership, your club is only the conduit for the collective transactions of all members. If it earns profits through dividends, interest and capital gains, those are divided up and reported each year according to each person's share of the total. These "realized earnings," whether or not you received the cash, create a taxable event. You are liable for the taxes on your share.

At the end of each calendar year, a partnership adds up the interest, dividends and capital gains, subtracts miscellaneous expenses and calculates the profit/loss earned during the year. This profit is then distributed to members, according to their percentage of ownership. As a partnership, an investment club is a pass-through entity—meaning it does not pay federal income taxes at the CLUB level. Each

For example: Let's say that no one in your club withdraws any money during the year. You all agree to leave your earnings on account to reinvest. You are still taxed on your share of the profits; just because you didn't withdraw those profits doesn't mean you can get around paying taxes on them.

The same rule applies if you withdraw more than you earn in any one year. Suppose that last year your share of club earnings was $400, but you have accumulated a fairly large amount of money over the years, so you withdraw $5,000. You are only taxed this year on your $400 earnings. The $5,000 withdrawal is a different matter. The sum of deposits you have made in the club plus earnings you have paid taxes on is your tax basis in the club. Any withdrawal less than your tax basis is tax free. Any amount over your tax basis is taxed as a long-term capital gain as long as the club is more than one year old. Most states that collect an income tax duplicate the federal rules somewhat, although some states have different rules for reporting income. Be sure to check with your state taxing agency for any special rules.

Also, the rules for taxation and treatment of withdrawals apply to individual accounts only. If your investment club account is part of an IRA or other tax-deferred retirement account, special penalties and taxes may apply to withdrawals.[10] Your treasurer should be clear on how a limited partnership is treated differently than a general partnership for tax purposes.

So the club has to file paperwork and so do I.

Correct. Partnerships must file Form 1065 along with a Schedule K-1 for each member.

Each member will receive their portion of dividends, interest, capital gains/losses and expenses on their personal K-1. This information is then transferred to the appropriate lines on their personal tax returns. The K-1 provides direction for placement of these items.

The forms/schedules above are for federal taxes. The club treasurer may also be required to file state, local and intangible property tax returns as well—and that's for each state and locality in which one of your members may reside. For these reasons, many clubs hire a CPA to help out at tax time. You may also opt to go outside for accounting assistance if your club has been formed as a corporation or other business entity with more complex tax requirements.

Form 1065

Figure 6-07 is a sample of Form 1065 (U.S. Partnership Return of Income), which reports profits and losses of the partnership. The key word here is reports. Once again, the partnership itself is not paying taxes. Rather, it is advising the government of its activity. The partnership passes any profits or losses, whether or not distributed, to the individual members who then pay any applicable taxes.

Schedule D, Form 1065

Capital gain income and loss are reported on Schedule D. See Figure 6-08. This information applies only to assets sold during the tax year. Short-term gains/losses pertain to assets held for one year or less. Long-term gains/losses are reported on assets held for more than one year.

Schedule K-1

This form, shown in Figure 6-09, reports the Partner's Share of Income. The club treasurer fills out one K-1 for each member. Each member should receive a copy of his or her own K-1. Individual members use this information to fill out their own tax returns.

*Internal Club
Year-End Documents*

The club treasurer and assistant treasurer prepare reports to assist individual members in filing their tax returns. Club accounting software cuts the time and eliminates the drudgery formerly associated with this duty. Complete details are found in the *NAIC Investment Club Accounting Handbook* and won't be reprinted here, but you should become acquainted with the forms themselves.

Shortly after the books are closed each year, you can expect to receive your club's Income and Expense Statement, a Balance Sheet and a Distribution of Earnings Statement.

Form 1065

Department of the Treasury
Internal Revenue Service

U.S. Return of Partnership Income

For calendar year 2003, or tax year beginning ...., 2003, and ending ...., 20..... .
► **See separate instructions.**

OMB No. 1545-0099

2003

A Principal business activity	Use the IRS label. Other-wise, print or type.	Name of partnership	D Employer identification number
B Principal product or service		Number, street, and room or suite no. If a P.O. box, see page 14 of the instructions.	E Date business started
C Business code number		City or town, state, and ZIP code	F Total assets (see page 14 of the instructions) $

G Check applicable boxes: **(1)** ☐ Initial return **(2)** ☐ Final return **(3)** ☐ Name change **(4)** ☐ Address change **(5)** ☐ Amended return

H Check accounting method: **(1)** ☐ Cash **(2)** ☐ Accrual **(3)** ☐ Other (specify) ► ....

I Number of Schedules K-1. Attach one for each person who was a partner at any time during the tax year ► ....

Caution: *Include **only** trade or business income and expenses on lines 1a through 22 below. See the instructions for more information.*

Income

1a Gross receipts or sales	**1a**		
b Less returns and allowances	**1b**	**1c**	
2 Cost of goods sold (Schedule A, line 8)		**2**	
3 Gross profit. Subtract line 2 from line 1c		**3**	
4 Ordinary income (loss) from other partnerships, estates, and trusts *(attach schedule)*		**4**	
5 Net farm profit (loss) *(attach Schedule F (Form 1040))*		**5**	
6 Net gain (loss) from Form 4797, Part II, line 18		**6**	
7 Other income (loss) *(attach schedule)*		**7**	
8 **Total income (loss).** Combine lines 3 through 7		**8**	

Deductions (see page 15 of the instructions for limitations)

9 Salaries and wages (other than to partners) (less employment credits)		**9**	
10 Guaranteed payments to partners		**10**	
11 Repairs and maintenance		**11**	
12 Bad debts		**12**	
13 Rent		**13**	
14 Taxes and licenses		**14**	
15 Interest		**15**	
16a Depreciation (if required, attach Form 4562)	**16a**		
b Less depreciation reported on Schedule A and elsewhere on return	**16b**	**16c**	
17 Depletion **(Do not deduct oil and gas depletion.)**		**17**	
18 Retirement plans, etc.		**18**	
19 Employee benefit programs		**19**	
20 Other deductions *(attach schedule)*		**20**	
21 **Total deductions.** Add the amounts shown in the far right column for lines 9 through 20		**21**	
22 **Ordinary income (loss)** from trade or business activities. Subtract line 21 from line 8		**22**	

Sign Here

Under penalties of perjury, I declare that I have examined this return, including accompanying schedules and statements, and to the best of my knowledge and belief, it is true, correct, and complete. Declaration of preparer (other than general partner or limited liability company member) is based on all information of which preparer has any knowledge.

► _____
Signature of general partner or limited liability company member

► _____
Date

May the IRS discuss this return with the preparer shown below (see instructions)? ☐ Yes ☐ No

Paid Prepareris Use Only

Preparer's signature		Date	Check if self-employed ► ☐	Preparer's SSN or PTIN
Firm's name (or yours if self-employed), address, and ZIP code	►		EIN ►	
			Phone no. ( )	

For Paperwork Reduction Act Notice, see separate instructions.   Cat. No. 11390Z   Form **1065** (2003)

FIGURE 6-07: FORM 1065 (U.S. PARTNERSHIP RETURN OF INCOME)

SCHEDULE D
(Form 1065)

Department of the Treasury
Internal Revenue Service

Capital Gains and Losses

▶ Attach to Form 1065.

OMB No. 1545-0099

2003

Name of partnership

Employer identification number

Part I — Short-Term Capital Gains and Losses—Assets Held 1 Year or Less

(a) Description of property (e.g., 100 shares of "Z" Co.)	(b) Date acquired (month, day, year)	(c) Date sold (month, day, year)	(d) Sales price (see instructions)	(e) Cost or other basis (see instructions)	(f) Gain or (loss) for the entire year Subtract (e) from (d)	(g) Post-May 5, 2003, gain or (loss) *(See below)
1						

2 Short-term capital gain from installment sales from Form 6252, line 26 or 37 . .	**2**	
3 Short-term capital gain (loss) from like-kind exchanges from Form 8824 . . .	**3**	
4 Partnership's share of net short-term capital gain (loss), including specially allocated short-term capital gains (losses), from other partnerships, estates, and trusts . . .	**4**	
5a Combine lines 1 through 4 in column (g). Enter here and on Form 1065, Schedule K, line 4d(1)	**5a**	
5b **Net short-term capital gain or (loss).** Combine lines 1 through 4 in column (f). Enter here and on Form 1065, Schedule K, line 4d(2) or 7	**5b**	

Part II — Long-Term Capital Gains and Losses—Assets Held More Than 1 Year

(a) Description of property (e.g., 100 shares of "Z" Co.)	(b) Date acquired (month, day, year)	(c) Date sold (month, day, year)	(d) Sales price (see instructions)	(e) Cost or other basis (see instructions)	(f) Gain or (loss) for the entire year Subtract (e) from (d)	(g) Post-May 5, 2003, gain or (loss) *(See below)
6						

7 Long-term capital gain from installment sales from Form 6252, line 26 or 37 . .	**7**	
8 Long-term capital gain (loss) from like-kind exchanges from Form 8824 . . .	**8**	
9 Partnership's share of net long-term capital gain (loss), including specially allocated long-term capital gains (losses), from other partnerships, estates, and trusts . .	**9**	
10 Capital gain distributions	**10**	
11 Combine lines 6 through 10 in column (g). Enter here and on Form 1065, Schedule K, line 4e(1) or 7	**11**	
12 **Net long-term capital gain or (loss).** Combine lines 6 through 10 in column (f). Enter here and on Form 1065, Schedule K, line 4e(2) or 7	**12**	

*Note: Include in column (g) all gains and losses from column (f) from sales, exchanges, or conversions (including installment payments received) **after** May 5, 2003. However, **do not** include gain attributable to unrecaptured section 1250 gain, a "collectibles gain or loss" (as defined on page 3) or the eligible gain on qualified small business stock (see page 3).

For Paperwork Reduction Act Notice, see the Instructions for Form 1065.   Cat. No. 11393G   Schedule D (Form 1065) 2003

FIGURE 6-08: SCHEDULE D, FORM 1065

6511

OMB No. 1545-0099

20**03**

SCHEDULE K-1
(Form 1065)
Department of the Treasury
Internal Revenue Service

Partner's Share of Income, Credits, Deductions, etc.
▶ See separate instructions.

For calendar year 2003 or tax year beginning   , 2003, and ending   , 20

Partner's identifying number ▶

Partnership's identifying number ▶

Partner's name, address, and ZIP code

Partnership's name, address, and ZIP code

A This partner is a ☐ general partner ☐ limited partner
☐ limited liability company member

B What type of entity is this partner? ▶ ....

C Is this partner a ☐ domestic or a ☐ foreign partner?

	(i) Before change or termination	**(ii)** End of year

D Enter partner's percentage of:

Profit sharing . . . . % .... %

Loss sharing . . . . % .... %

Ownership of capital . . . . % .... %

E IRS Center where partnership filed return:

F Partner's share of liabilities (see instructions):

Nonrecourse . . . . $ ....

Qualified nonrecourse financing . $ ....

Other . . . . $ ....

G Tax shelter registration number . ▶ ....

H Check here if this partnership is a publicly traded partnership as defined in section 469(k)(2) . . . . . ☐

I Check applicable boxes: **(1)** ☐ Final K-1 **(2)** ☐ Amended K-1

J Analysis of partner's capital account:

(a) Capital account at beginning of year	**(b)** Capital contributed during year	**(c)** Partner's share of lines 3, 4, and 7, Form 1065, Schedule M-2	**(d)** Withdrawals and distributions	**(e)** Capital account at end of year (combine columns (a) through (d))
			( )	

	(a) Distributive share item		**(b)** Amount	**(c)** 1040 filers enter the amount in column (b) on:
Income (Loss)	**1** Ordinary income (loss) from trade or business activities . . .	**1**		See page 6 of Partner's Instructions for Schedule K-1 (Form 1065).
	2 Net income (loss) from rental real estate activities	**2**		
	3 Net income (loss) from other rental activities	**3**		
	4 Portfolio income (loss):			
	a Interest income	**4a**		Form 1040, line 8a
	b (1) Qualified dividends	**4b(1)**		Form 1040, line 9b
	(2) Total ordinary dividends	**4b(2)**		Form 1040, line 9a
	c Royalty income	**4c**		Sch. E, Part I, line 4
	d (1) Net short-term capital gain (loss) (post-May 5, 2003) . . .	**4d(1)**		Sch. D, line 5, col. (g)
	(2) Net short-term capital gain (loss) (entire year)	**4d(2)**		Sch. D, line 5, col. (f)
	e (1) Net long-term capital gain (loss) (post-May 5, 2003) . . .	**4e(1)**		Sch. D, line 12, col. (g)
	(2) Net long-term capital gain (loss) (entire year)	**4e(2)**		Sch. D, line 12, col. (f)
	f Other portfolio income (loss) *(attach schedule)*	**4f**		
	5 Guaranteed payments to partner	**5**		See pages 6 and 7 of Partner's Instructions for Schedule K-1 (Form 1065).
	6a Net section 1231 gain (loss) (post-May 5, 2003)	**6a**		
	b Net section 1231 gain (loss) (entire year)	**6b**		
	7 Other income (loss) *(attach schedule)*	**7**		
Deduc-tions	**8** Charitable contributions (see instructions) *(attach schedule)* . .	**8**		Sch. A, line 15 or 16
	9 Section 179 expense deduction	**9**		See page 8 of Partner's Instructions for Schedule K-1 (Form 1065).
	10 Deductions related to portfolio income *(attach schedule)* . . .	**10**		
	11 Other deductions *(attach schedule)*	**11**		
Credits	**12a** Low-income housing credit: **(1)** From section 42(j)(5) partnerships	**12a(1)**		Form 8586, line 5
	(2) Other than on line 12a(1)	**12a(2)**		
	b Qualified rehabilitation expenditures related to rental real estate activities	**12b**		See page 9 of Partner's Instructions for Schedule K-1 (Form 1065).
	c Credits (other than credits shown on lines 12a and 12b) related to rental real estate activities	**12c**		
	d Credits related to other rental activities	**12d**		
	13 Other credits	**13**		

For Paperwork Reduction Act Notice, see Instructions for Form 1065.

Cat. No. 11394R

Schedule K-1 (Form 1065) 2003

FIGURE 6-09: SCHEDULE K-1 (PARTNER'S SHARE OF INCOME)—PAGE 1

Schedule K-1 (Form 1065) 2003   Page **2**

	(a) Distributive share item	(b) Amount	(c) 1040 filers enter the amount in column (b) on:
Investment Interest	**14a** Interest expense on investment debts . . . . **b** (1) Investment income included on lines 4a, 4b(2), 4c, and 4f (2) Investment expenses included on line 10	14a 14b(1) 14b(2)	Form 4952, line 1 } See page 9 of Partner's Instructions for Schedule K-1 (Form 1065).
Self-employment	**15a** Net earnings (loss) from self-employment . . . . **b** Gross farming or fishing income . . . . **c** Gross nonfarm income	15a 15b 15c	Sch. SE, Section A or B } See page 9 of Partner's Instructions for Schedule K-1 (Form 1065).
Adjustments and Tax Preference Items	**16a** Depreciation adjustment on property placed in service after 1986 **b** Adjusted gain or loss . . . . **c** Depletion (other than oil and gas) . . . . **d** (1) Gross income from oil, gas, and geothermal properties . . (2) Deductions allocable to oil, gas, and geothermal properties **e** Other adjustments and tax preference items *(attach schedule)*	16a 16b 16c 16d(1) 16d(2) 16e	See pages 9 and 10 of Partner's Instructions for Schedule K-1 (Form 1065) and Instructions for Form 6251.
Foreign Taxes	**17a** Name of foreign country or U.S. possession ▶ . . . . **b** Gross income from all sources . . . . **c** Gross income sourced at partner level . . . . **d** Foreign gross income sourced at partnership level: (1) Passive . . . . (2) Listed categories *(attach schedule)* . . . . (3) General limitation . . . . **e** Deductions allocated and apportioned at partner level: (1) Interest expense . . . . (2) Other . . . . **f** Deductions allocated and apportioned at partnership level to foreign source income: (1) Passive . . . . (2) Listed categories *(attach schedule)* . . . . (3) General limitation . . . . **g** Total foreign taxes (check one): ▶ ☐ Paid ☐ Accrued . . . **h** Reduction in taxes available for credit *(attach schedule)* . . .	17b 17c 17d(1) 17d(2) 17d(3) 17e(1) 17e(2) 17f(1) 17f(2) 17f(3) 17g 17h	Form 1116, Part I Form 1116, Part II Form 1116, line 12
Other	**18** Section 59(e)(2) expenditures: **a** Type ▶ . . . . **b** Amount . . . . **19** Tax-exempt interest income . . . . **20** Other tax-exempt income . . . . **21** Nondeductible expenses . . . . **22** Distributions of money (cash and marketable securities) . . . **23** Distributions of property other than money . . . . **24** Recapture of low-income housing credit: **a** From section 42(j)(5) partnerships . . . . **b** Other than on line 24a	18b 19 20 21 22 23 24a 24b	} See page 10 of Partner's Instructions for Schedule K-1 (Form 1065). Form 1040, line 8b } See page 10 of Partner's Instructions for Schedule K-1 (Form 1065). } Form 8611, line 8
Supplemental Information	**25** Supplemental information required to be reported separately to each partner *(attach additional schedules if more space is needed):*		

⊛   **Schedule K-1 (Form 1065) 2003**

FIGURE 6-09: SCHEDULE K-1 (PARTNER'S SHARE OF INCOME)—PAGE 2

Summary

The NAIC Accounting System was designed with the inexperienced bookkeeper in mind. It provides all the information required by the club, its individual members and governmental agencies.

Refer to the *NAIC Investment Club Accounting Handbook* for assistance on pretty much every type of transaction you'll encounter. Download a copy of *NAIC Club Accounting Software* by visiting the NAIC Web Site—www.better-investing.org—or make use of NAIC Online Club Accounting at www.NAIC-club.com.

The treasurer is ultimately responsible for club record keeping. However, it is highly recommended that each member of the club become somewhat familiar with the process. Each member should also be prepared to audit the work of the treasurer if asked to do so.

The treasurer maintains records of the club's financial affairs. The assistant treasurer maintains records of the members' interests, or members' share ownership of the club's assets.

Your club is an investment making enterprise issuing partnership units, and selling these to a limited clientele. Using the Valuation Unit System, the club will calculate the value of one unit the same way a mutual fund computes the Net Asset Value (NAV): by dividing the dollar value of club assets by the number of Valuation Units issued by the club.

The Valuation Unit System permits members to increase or decrease their monthly investment or to make partial withdrawals. It also anticipates changes in membership, allowing new members to come in fresh with their minimum monthly payment, rather than having to "buy out" the interest of the departing member.

Prior to each monthly meeting, a Valuation Statement is prepared by the club treasurer.

The Valuation Statement displays the securities owned by the club and their total current value, the amount of cash on hand, the current value of one Valuation Unit and the number of Valuation Units that can be purchased with $10.00.

The club treasurer should become familiar with the *NAIC Investment Club Accounting Handbook* and/or the proper use of *NAIC Club Accounting Software*. All members must know what triggers a taxable event and how the IRS treats capital gains distributions.

Figure 6-02 lists the five possible withdrawal options for a full withdrawal. Figure 6-03 lists the five possible withdrawal options for a partial withdrawal.

The general provisions for a withdrawal from an individual's capital account should be firmly set in the club's partnership agreement.

The Valuation Unit System was set up with the clear expectation that member rotation was inevitable, and therefore makes new member initiation painless to the pocketbook.

To ensure that people interested in joining have a clear understanding of the club's goals and its strategies to achieve them, most clubs have an effective screening/ initiation process.

Prospective members should have a chance to review the club's partnership agreement and operating procedures. They should also be clear on the club's requirements for minimum meeting attendance and annual number of stock and/or educational presentations. Many clubs have a probationary period during which candidates attend meetings and even participate.

Some clubs appoint a membership officer who creates a prospective member packet. Figure 6-05 shows some items that may be included. In addition, this member will be assigned to serve as a mentor to candidates, guiding them through the internship process.

There are very few restrictions and requirements for a club. Don't advertise. Revise the partnership agreement and operating procedures and be sure to notify NAIC of membership changes when necessary.

Listed in Figure 6-06 are various Internet sites to find investment club accounting information, advice and links.

The partnership does not pay federal income taxes, but reports the overall results to the IRS, as well as each member's portion of the total. Club members are personally liable for payment of their share of the club's income/loss.

IRS Form 1065 (U.S. Partnership Return of Income) reports profits and losses of the partnership. Capital gain income and loss are reported on Schedule D. Schedule K-1 reports the Partner's Share of Income. The club treasurer fills out one K-1 for each member. The treasurer mails the original copy of the 1065, Schedule D and all K-1's to the appropriate IRS Center and retains a copy for club records. Each individual member receives their personal K-1 to use for informational purposes when filing their own tax returns. Member should keep their copies and not mail them in with their personal tax returns.

The club treasurer and assistant treasurer prepare internal reports to assist members in filing their individual tax returns. These include the club's Income and Expense Statement, a Balance Sheet and a Distribution of Earnings Statement.

Chapter Notes

[1] Robert A. Burger, *NAIC Investment Club Accounting Handbook* (National Association of Investors Corporation, 1995) 2. The Handbook is used as a source of additional general information for this chapter.

[2] Thomas E. O'Hara and Kenneth S. Janke, Sr., *Starting and Running a Profitable Investment Club* (New York: Times Books, 1998) 203-204.

[3] NAIC Computer Group, "NAIC Investment Club Accounting 1999 Teacher Training Workshop," 5.

[4] O'Hara and Janke 205.

[5] Burger 14-16.

[6] "1999 Teacher Training" 9-10.

[7] "1999 Teacher Training" 11-12.

[8] Burger, 38.

[9] Douglas Gerlach and Angele McQuade, "Finding New Club Members," Better Investing April 2002: 30-32.

[10] O'Hara and Janke 215-216.

CHAPTER SEVEN:

Starting to Invest with Your Club

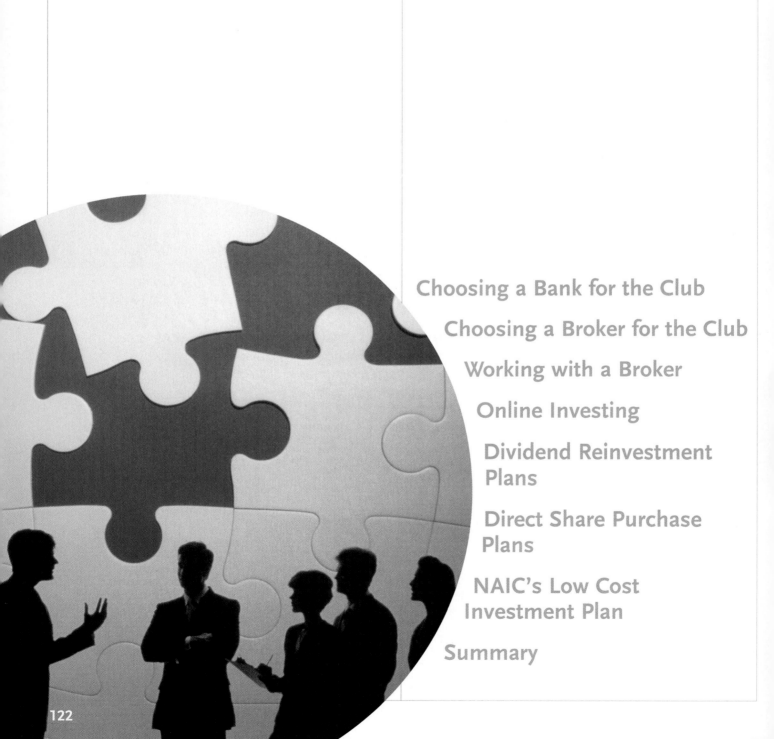

Choosing a Bank for the Club

Choosing a Broker for the Club

Working with a Broker

Online Investing

Dividend Reinvestment Plans

Direct Share Purchase Plans

NAIC's Low Cost Investment Plan

Summary

Perhaps we put the cart before the horse. Chapter 6 discussed tax payments. On what? Your fledgling club hasn't been around long enough to pay any.

Chapter 7 and Chapter 8 will begin to make you and the IRS happy by showing you how to establish good investing practices. We start by discussing where and with whom to put your money. This is not to be confused with stock picking, which is the subject of many other NAIC materials. Rather, we will explore your options for parking the club's dollars, stretching them to the max and performing due diligence prior to investing them. These are the "little things" that eventually put bigger numbers on the ledger next to your name.

Choosing a Bank for the Club

Each member of the club brings a check to the monthly meeting. Then, at that meeting, you mutually determine what to do with the pooled money. The club treasurer can endorse member checks over to the club's broker, and can also write checks on the brokerage account to pay club bills.

However, you may also consider establishing a business account at a local bank where you can deposit member checks, turn them around and send one club check to the broker, parking the leftover funds until needed.

Although you may be on a first-name basis with the tellers at the local bank, you may be unaware of the bank's services pertaining to a group such as an investment club. And you may be totally unfamiliar with other types of financial institutions. Figure 7-01 presents a brief primer on the three that can handle your club's banking needs:

FIGURE 7-01: FINANCIAL INSTITUTIONS. PRIMER

INSTITUTION	DESCRIPTION
Commercial Bank	Commercial banks are regulated by state or federal charter. Federally chartered banks are members of the Federal Reserve system or the Federal Deposit Insurance Corporation (FDIC), which insures deposits up to $100,000. Banks can loan money and offer checking and savings accounts, money market accounts, certificates of deposit and other services.
Thrifts	The term "savings and loan" (S&L) has taken it on the chin since the 1980s, but the Savings & Loan Insurance Corporation insures individual deposits up to $100,000. S&Ls handle deposits and make personal loans.
Credit Unions	Credit unions are non-profit organizations that are generally accessible to people of a single group or occupation, such as teachers. Because they don't pay federal income taxes, they can often offer higher interest rates on savings and lower interest rates on loans. Credit unions are insured by the NCUA (National Credit Union Administration).

What about just putting all our money in the brokerage account? Doesn't that eliminate one potential hassle?

Perhaps. Perhaps not. There are good pros and cons to your question. We'll save the positives—like check-writing privileges—for the next section on brokerages. Just keep in mind that the club is going to need its money for more than investing. Even if it's just sending out for pizzas or buying pencils, you may find that having all your available funds in a brokerage, especially one that doesn't have a local office or ATM, may limit your immediate access to cash.

What about online banking?

If you open an account at the bank on the corner that also offers online services, you've got the best of both worlds: full electronic banking along with the personal service and immediate access to cash money.

Many large national banks offer online banking with a range of ancillary services. It is convenient, secure and efficient. Once again, though—and maybe this is an inconsequential issue to you— you may want to investigate how it compares with your local bank for getting that pizza money when you need it.

There are lots of people who swear by electronic transacting and enjoy telling the rest of us to stop thinking of banking as Jimmy Stewart in *"It's a Wonderful Life."* Maybe so.

At any rate, you've got a lot to consider, even for a seemingly small matter like opening up a business account with its primary purpose as a funnel to deposit lots of individual checks and kick out one club check each month.

Here are a few considerations in addition to those already mentioned:

- **Fees.** They're all over the place. You want to avoid monthly service charges, maintenance fees, check writing fees, whatever fees. Ask and compare. It's a buyer's market.

- **Minimum Balance.** The lowest minimum is the best. How much money you leave parked there should be your call, not their requirement. Think about where your money could be making more money.

- **Interest.** It's a small matter these days, but a few percent could add up. Interest-bearing checking accounts for businesses may not be an option. Look into money market accounts or CDs if you plan to have balances that you can leave

in there to obtain the higher rates.

- **Personal Service.** If one of the club members has a long-standing relationship at a local institution, it may waive certain requirements to get your business and be a good neighbor. If a member already belongs to a credit union, perhaps the club can be "grandfathered" in, bypassing restrictions. Note that the member who belongs may be required to co-sign any club checks.

Choosing a Broker for the Club

Choosing a bank was the easy part. Making a determination as to where and with whom to commit your investment dollars takes a bit more thought. We can't do the thinking for you, but can make the process a bit less fretful than the last time you bought a major appliance.

There are three types of brokerage houses that will transact the purchase and sale of securities for you: full-service, discount and deep-discount brokers.

What about an online broker?

This has become a misnomer in the past few years. The designation of "online broker" more accurately refers to the way in which the trade is being transacted (i.e. executed online) rather than the type of broker that's doing the transacting.

A majority of brokerage firms offer online access to account information and transaction abilities. In addition, most brokers can be contacted via computer and their fees may or may not be adjusted because the trade is being executed electronically. To say that you make investment transactions online is therefore more accurate.

What, then, are the differences in the three types?

In this section we'll take you through the basic structural differences. In the next section, we'll explore the differences in actually using each type of broker. Your basic decision will be the trade-off between transaction costs versus services. If you require more services and support, you will pay more. If you want lower transaction costs and can live with minimal services, you will pay less!

The Full-Service Broker

You've seen the Boy Scout who walks the little old lady across the street? The full-service broker pulls up in a taxicab and rides in the back seat with her.

Financially speaking, full-service brokers are your 24/7 guardian angels. They will feel empowered—and even obligated—to call you before you call them, and offer recommendations based on

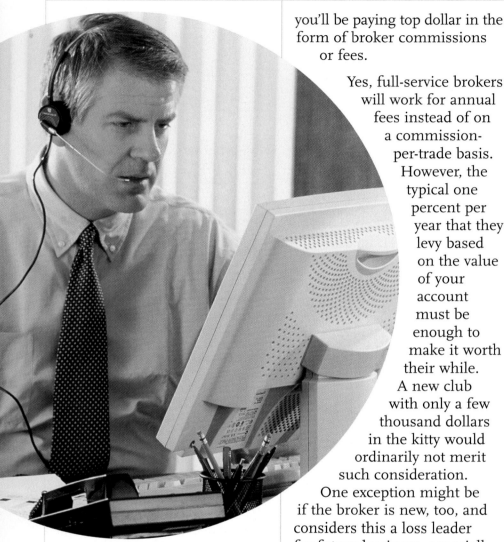

you'll be paying top dollar in the form of broker commissions or fees.

Yes, full-service brokers will work for annual fees instead of on a commission-per-trade basis. However, the typical one percent per year that they levy based on the value of your account must be enough to make it worth their while. A new club with only a few thousand dollars in the kitty would ordinarily not merit such consideration. One exception might be if the broker is new, too, and considers this a loss leader for future business, especially the prospect of landing the individual accounts of club members.

The Discount Broker

Now we move to the category created after 1975, when the SEC did away with fixed commissions. The discount broker came into being and swept through the industry like a sandstorm, gobbling up existing full-service accounts and making it possible for

virtually anyone to become an individual investor.

At the time, discount brokers were set up simply to make trades. No free research, no reports, no phone calls with hot tips—but no high-end commissions, either.

And then, two things happened. As clients became more knowledgeable about the market, they demanded more services for the same or similar fees. Thus, discounters such as Charles Schwab quietly made their research more accessible and their non-commission-based sales force more helpful.

As these firms moved closer toward full-service status, the gap they left was filled by very willing start-ups who set up shop on the Internet, offering almost nothing and charging the same.

The Deep-Discount Broker

"You get what you pay for" was never more appropriate. With a few keystrokes, the investor became able to buy and sell securities for dollars per transaction. Deep discounters thrived because the do-it-yourself investor wanted no more than an electronic conduit to the trading floor and companies like Ameritrade were born to provide it.

Deep discounters, like discount brokers, execute buy and sell orders with great speed. Due to their bare-bones operation, they

the tremendous research resources that their firm has at hand. Your club can be provided with as much of this research as it wishes. The broker, upon request, can offer input and advice concerning a stock the club is studying.

But like that taxicab, the meter is running. Not hourly, mind you, like an attorney or a plumber. But for all the research and reports and recommendations,

can do so at great reductions in cost. Some charge a flat per-share commission; others offer a sliding scale based on the number of shares traded.

Working with a Broker[1]

So how do we find a broker with whom we can begin a mutually satisfying relationship?

First, you need to find a broker who knows a thing or two about investment clubs. Second, you want someone to advise you, not to sell you. One of the prime turn-offs of full-service brokers is their reliance on commission-based products.

So consider cost. Minimum commissions are often the same for both major discount and full-service brokers. Once you begin investing in larger blocks, the discounts become more significant.

In the fourth or fifth year of operation, a club may reach a crossroad. Some clubs "move up" to a full-service broker to gain another perspective on the market, as well as to broaden investment choices. On the other hand, some clubs become more confident in their ability to make good decisions without the advice of a broker, and switch to, or remain with, a deep-discount firm.

Meanwhile, how do we begin?

Whether you select a full-service or a discount firm, all members of the club have to sign an agreement when your account is opened. The agreement varies from firm to firm, but in all cases authorization must be given to the designated individuals to place buy and sell orders.

Let's say we sign up with a full-service broker in hopes of getting exactly that: full service. What can we really expect?

If you select a full-service broker, remember the most essential and necessary element in the relationship: the broker must understand your investment philosophy and help you to achieve your goals. If the broker tries to force decisions on you, the relationship won't work.

As part of the relationship, your broker should be willing to provide your club with extra services not necessary for individual customers: custody of securities, dividend collection and forwarding of stockholder notices. Some brokers want a service charge for these extras. The broker probably also expects that several, and possibly all, of your members will eventually open personal accounts with him or her.

Respect the broker's objectives. Remember, the broker is in business to make money. During the hours the market is open, brokers are consumed with placing buy and sell orders or soliciting such orders

from customers. Ask if there is a particular time, either early morning or late afternoon, that is the best time to talk.

Also, out of respect for the broker's requirements, don't expect him or her to deal with more than one individual representing the club; usually that's the financial partner. About twenty-four hours before the club's meeting, ask the broker for any recent information on stocks in the club's portfolio, as well as stocks being studied for possible purchase.

Shouldn't a full-service broker be telling us what to buy?

No, that's your club's decision. However, once the decision

has been made, you may certainly ask your broker's opinion before placing an order. If he/she has valid objections, you should listen carefully and then poll club members before proceeding.

Information obtained from your broker in advance of the meeting should be recorded and shared with club members before any investment actions are taken. As soon as possible after the meeting, the club's contact person should place the authorized order with the broker. Don't hesitate to call during trading hours with a buy or sell order; that's the best time. However, if you want to talk at length with your broker, wait until after hours

and try to schedule such discussions in advance.

When your club has selected a stock to study, ask the broker for copies of Standard & Poor's or Value Line sheets. Be fair in requesting material from the full-service broker in order to minimize the expense of handling your account. There is no need to order more than the two to four Standard & Poor's sheets required for next month's reports.

What about calling the broker for prices?

Try and confine the use of your full-service broker to obtaining that which you can't get anywhere else. The most recent prices are available continuously on various cable TV stations as well as on the Internet. Closing prices from the previous trading session are listed in your local newspaper. Your broker can't do any better.

What is the correct procedure once we've decided what to buy?

Your financial officer should transmit one check to your broker, having deposited members' payments in the club's bank account. Be prompt; payment must reach the broker within three business days following issuance of the buy order.

The broker is subject to a fine if he/she fails to require on-time payment. If you don't meet the deadline, your broker could be required to place your club on a restricted list and possibly be forced to collect funds from you in advance of accepting your orders.

Shouldn't the broker be attending our meetings? Isn't that part of the "full service"?

You and your fellow club members are in business to learn by doing, not to defer to the opinions of others you consider more knowledgeable than yourselves. Invite the broker to your annual meeting only.

The broker should be asked to offer suggestions on your study program for the months ahead. However, remember that you started your club to make your own decisions. The broker should be asked only to comment generally, and should not be expected to assume responsibility for your investing success. That's your task.

Online Investing

Many of my trader friends swear by online investing. What can you tell me about it?

The growth of online investing resources, data and information is a positive development benefiting many investors. Here are some of NAIC's guidelines when using online resources for investing:

- **Take your time and understand the basics.** Many investors jump into buying and selling stocks online before they know the basics of investing. There is a big difference between online investing and online trading. Online investing requires research, knowledge of stocks and a clear reasoning why you are buying or selling along with the associated risks. Online trading refers to the quick buying and selling of stocks, and should be left to professionals. Make sure you are comfortable with investing before doing so in the lightning-fast world of cyber-space.

- **Use the Internet as an educational pool of information, but don't drown in it!** The Internet offers investors a wealth of valuable investment information and education. To a person learning about investing, it brings a worldwide financial library to your desktop. However, the available information is so vast that one can easily get caught up in the overload! See Chapter 10 for directories of helpful Web sites, and try using Internet search engines to find Web sites that will provide the specific information you need.

- **Use online broker demonstration sites before making your first trade.** Many online brokers offer a demo area that allows you to walk through the process of purchasing or selling stocks online before you sign up. Use these services as an educational process before making any commitment.

- **Be sure you know about all fees and costs.** Investing online can look like a real deal. Research all the costs involved before signing up. Determine if there is a minimum account amount required, as well as extra costs for mailings, annual fees, selling stocks, etc.

- **Know where to go for consumer help.** If you have difficulties with an online broker, report your problem or concern to the brokerage firm involved, the National Association of Securities Dealers (NASD), the Securities and Exchange Commission (SEC) or your State Securities Office.

Dividend Reinvestment Plans

Building wealth through dividend reinvestment is one of the most fundamental messages NAIC has been spreading across the nation for over a half-century. It involves the use of two of NAIC's investment principles: regular investing and the reinvestment of earnings. To this day, it remains one of the most popular and cost-effective ways of building wealth over the long term. In fact, some clubs may not even retain a broker for the first few years because they concentrate their investments almost exclusively on stocks with dividend reinvestment plans.

Are dividends really important anymore?

We'll let NAIC Chairman Tom O'Hara handle that one. "Dividends haven't been getting much attention [in] recent years," he said in late 2000, "but the day will come again when they will be just as important, or even more important, than stock price appreciation. So don't forget about them."[2]

And we can reinvest dividends paid out by our club stocks automatically?

That's right, you reinvest by enrolling in a dividend-paying company's Dividend Reinvestment Plan (DRP, commonly pronounced drip). Instead of receiving a quarterly payout in cash, the dividend is used to purchase more shares.

With no commission?

That's often the case, yes. If there are any commissions at all, they're usually reduced. And some companies even purchase the new shares for you at lower-than-market prices.

Does the entire amount (after fees) go to purchase shares?

Yes. You're credited with fractional shares for any cash left over after whole shares are purchased.

It sounds like a great system to dollar cost average.

That's the perfect way of looking at it.

How can we find out which companies offer DRPs?

Some Web sites that offer this information are:
www.netstockdirect.com
www.dripinvestor.com
www.dripcentral.com

What else do I need to know?

This is a general discussion so we can't get into every nook and cranny here, but you'll definitely want to ask about any fees involved, and be sure that your club treasurer keeps accurate records. Reinvested dividends are taxable in the same manner as dividends paid directly to shareholders. In addition, while many plans do not have commission or administrative charges, the pro-rata amount may be added to the dividends when reported to you on form 1099 at the conclusion of the calendar year as required by the IRS.

Direct Share Purchase Plans

Also known as Direct Stock Plans, a DSP offers another way to avoid brokers—and

possibly commissions—altogether. While DRPs are used to reinvest dividends of shares already owned in a company, the DSP is set up to facilitate the purchase of initial company shares.

What's the advantage of a DSP for our club?

Aside from the obvious monetary benefits of buying directly from the company, it's a great way for your club to get its feet wet by being able to buy a minimal number of shares in that company.

And the disadvantages?

Because you're not going through a broker, you may have to hold the stock certificates

yourself. Normally, your stocks are held in street name, meaning that the brokerage holds the certificates (and thereby the shares of stock) for you. It's just more paperwork, but as you're not, theoretically, doing a lot of buying and selling within the club, you shouldn't mind the added record keeping.

If and when you do sell, holding the certificate may cause a time lag in the transaction in two ways. First, you'll have to send the certificate back to the company for redemption. Second, some companies set specific times (e.g. once a month) to sell off DSP shares, further delaying the trade.

In any event, be aware of how each company's plan works and you'll avoid costly surprises later.

NAIC's Low Cost Investment Plan

Speaking of cost, the Low Cost Investment Plan offered by NAIC is an easy and inexpensive way for clubs to purchase stocks and invest regularly.

What is the NAIC Low Cost Investment Plan?

The Low Cost Plan was established to help NAIC members start a cost-effective lifetime investment program in companies offering a dividend reinvestment or optional cash purchase plan.

Is this a brokerage service?

No. NAIC has joined the dividend reinvestment or optional cash purchase plans of participating companies (see the NAIC Web Site— www.better-investing.org—for a current list) and makes stock purchases within those plans with the funds sent by NAIC members. NAIC acts as a conduit for its members to gain access to the company plans. All money received by NAIC is invested in the selected company except for a one-time setup charge. Companies on the list are not to be considered as endorsed or recommended for purchase by NAIC. Investors should make their own review and analysis of companies of interest before making an investment decision.

When are stocks purchased?

Since NAIC is not a broker, purchases are made at the time and price determined by the company's transfer agent. These investments are made regularly for each company, either monthly or quarterly, and the price is the prevailing price at the time of the transaction.

How long does it take?

The initial process takes approximately 8 weeks from the time your check arrives at NAIC until you can transact directly with the company's transfer agent to purchase more stock. Companies that purchase quarterly take longer.

Can we buy more than one share?

You are limited on the initial investment to purchase the minimum required to establish the account. In most cases, this will be one share. However, some companies require more than one share and this will be specified on the list of participating companies.

Can we purchase companies that are NOT on the list?

Only the companies on the list are participants. NAIC must have the permission of the company before they are listed as a participant. The steps taken before a company is added depend on factors agreeable to NAIC, the company and the transfer agent. NAIC also requires that the company have a five-year record of public trading and offering a dividend reinvestment or optional cash purchase plan.

How does the club enroll?

Enrollment forms are available in *Better Investing* magazine and on the NAIC Web Site.

Summary

You need a business account at a local financial institution where you can deposit member checks, turn them around, send one club check to the broker and then park the left-over funds until needed. Commercial banks, thrifts and credit unions are three such institutions that can handle your club's banking needs.

Consider fees, minimum balance, interest and personal service when deciding on a bank.

There are three types of brokerage houses that will transact the purchase and sale of securities for you: full-service, discount and deep-discount brokers. Each has its own set of advantages and disadvantages, depending on your club's needs.

Find a broker who knows a thing or two about investment clubs and who will advise you, not sell you.

If you select a full-service broker, remember the most essential and necessary element in the relationship: the broker must understand your investment philosophy and help you to achieve your goals. If the broker tries to force decisions on you, the relationship won't work.

Follow these guidelines when using online investing resources: take your time and understand the basics; use the Internet as an educational pool of information, but don't drown in it; use online broker demonstration sites before making your first trade; be sure you know all fees and costs; and know where to go for consumer help.

The Dividend Reinvestment Plan and Direct Stock Plan are two ways to purchase shares of stock from companies and avoid broker commissions.

The Low Cost Investment Plan offered by NAIC is an easy and inexpensive way for clubs to purchase stocks and invest regularly.

Chapter Notes

[1] Much of this section is taken from Thomas E. O'Hara and Kenneth S. Janke, Sr., *Starting and Running a Profitable Investment Club* (New York: Times Books, 1998) 187-191.

[2] "A Chairman's Perspective on Dividends," *Better Investing* October 2000: 49

Finding Investment Information

The Need for Financial Information & Resources

In the previous chapter, you learned how brokers and bankers can actually—and perhaps surprisingly—be your financial friends. You also discovered how you can alleviate some of the labor by taking your dividends and "letting them ride" through dividend reinvestment plans.

It sounds too easy. I have a feeling I'm being set up.

If by that you're realizing that the investment process is not exactly the same as picking a song on a jukebox, you're right. Investing is a commitment of time as well as money, and although the amount of return on investment is never directly proportional to the amount of labor, slacking off on the due diligence is a set-up, all right—a set-up for failure.

The New York Stock Exchange and NASDAQ together are comprised of more than 8,000 issues. And there are just about as many magazines, talk shows and Web sites that upon first glance seem to be able to predict tomorrow with deadly accuracy and at the same time explain why yesterday's prediction was totally off the mark.

It therefore becomes your obligation as an active investment club member to separate the wheat from the chaff of information sources before doing the same for stocks under consideration by the club.

In this chapter, you'll be guided to such sources in a variety of places, from your local library to the companies themselves, including NAIC's *Better Investing* magazine, NAIC's Web Site and NAIC's Top 100 Stocks list. Much of the information is free. Certain expenses incurred in obtaining investing information, such as a newsletter subscription, may be tax deductible; be sure to do the proper research or consult your investment advisor to be sure.

Resources at Your Library

So much information is available without leaving home, just keystrokes away. It's no wonder, then, that a library card has become all but an artifact from some archaeological dig to the latest generation of investors That's a pity, and a mistake.

What can I find at the library that I can't just download?

A human being, for one thing. Librarians can be a fountain of knowledge on what's available and what's appropriate. They can help cut through the clutter of stuff out there and narrow in on your specific needs.

The art of investing isn't new. A book doesn't have to be a current best seller, or its author on *The Tonight Show* couch next to the zoo lady and this week's movie idol, to be the most valid source of information. The local librarian can be your guide to an undiscovered world of wisdom—a living, breathing search engine.

That said, most libraries are not tombs of tomes. They are up to date and state of the art. If you do want that current best seller, chances are they'll have it for free on their shelves at about the same time as the mall bookstore will have it for sale on theirs.

I have a confession to make: I already skipped down to Chapter 10, where I found lists of investing periodicals and newsletters. Can I "audition" them at the library to find the ones I want to subscribe to?

You'll probably find a lot of fellow investors with the same idea. *Value Line* and *Standard and Poor's Stock Reports* are particularly excellent sources of

the information you'll need to fill out an NAIC Stock Selection Guide. Try reading them at the library and using what you need for your club meetings.

Rediscover the library and you'll agree that it's an all-too-forgotten source of news, knowledge and advice.

Information Provided by Public Corporations

Public corporations (companies whose stock trade publicly) are required by law to disclose financial information and provide it to shareholders and to the general public. Your club treasurer should receive all such mailings and share them with interested members.

Here are brief thumbnails on the major reports available.

Annual Report

The annual report is an investor's primary source of financial intelligence about a company. Written by the company itself, the report offers information about the company, its products or services, its employees and customers and its future outlook.

While all annual reports are not alike, you will find the following in most of them:

- Corporate Profile
- Financial Highlights
- Letter to Shareholders
- Operational Overview

- Independent Auditor's Report
- Financial Statements and Notes
- Management Discussion/Analysis
- Description of Company Business
- Business Segment Information
- Listing of Directors and Officers
- Five-year Historical Financial Data[1]

Most annual reports will also include a notification of the company's annual meeting, and a proxy statement/card for voting on motions to be brought before the board of directors. As responsible owners of the company, you should consider it a club duty to return your proxies, which you can do easily by mail, phone or e-mail.

10-K Report

Much longer and more detailed than an annual report, Form 10-K must be filed annually (within 90 days after the close of the fiscal year) with the Securities and Exchange Commission. Professional analysts use it as an important research tool. Shareholders may receive the report free of charge upon request; there may be a charge to non-shareholders.[2] You can download a copy of any company's Form 10-K from the SEC Web site (www.sec.gov).

Corporate Quarterly Reports/10-Q Report

Shareholders may receive a quarterly report by mail, or be advised that it is available online at the company's Web site. (It can also be accessed on the SEC site noted above). These reports summarize activities in the most-recent quarter, including unaudited financial statements. The 10-Q is more detailed than the report provided to shareholders, and is filed with the SEC around 45 days after the close of each quarter.[3] It, too, is available on the SEC Web site.

Other Information

- When an important event occurs within a public company (e.g. an impending merger or acquisition, the sale or spin-off of a corporate division, the introduction of a new product), the news will be released to the public and to shareholders. Watch your mail for separate bulletins of this nature.

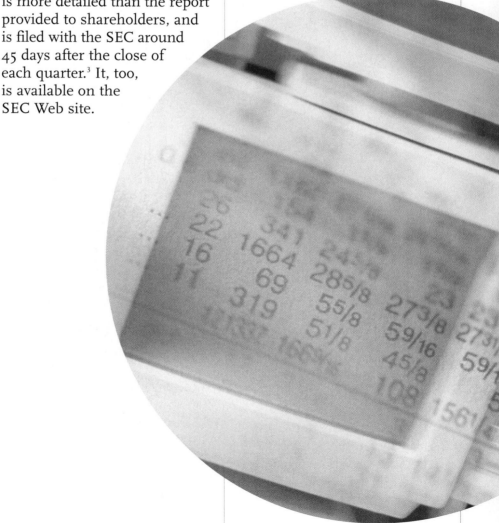

Brokerage Firm Research

In Chapter 7, a comparison of broker types revealed that clients of full-service houses are able to enjoy the full extent of their research services. Discounters also make a certain amount of research available upon request.

These reports may span multiple pages and include analyst recommendations. Full-service clients should ascertain whether the broker firm is making a market for the recommended stock or whether the firm was an underwriter on any recent stock offerings for that company. If so, the opinions expressed may be colored by such underlying factors.[5]

Brokerage firms also frequently sponsor free investment seminars. You'll come away with some good handouts on the fundamentals of stocks and funds. You'll also get pitched for your business, so let the investor beware.[6]

Finding It on the Internet

An NAIC survey conducted in 2002 indicated that over 94% of NAIC members owned a computer, and a growing number of members register at the NAIC Web Site (www.better-investing.org).

By setting up an account—which only requires a few pieces of information and no cost—NAIC members can use the "Search String" window to access just about every piece of information on the site. Search for published information by author, column or subject, or use key words to reference a host of subjects and areas of interest.

Users can also search the abundant archives of the I-Club-List for information and comments from other NAIC members. Two message forums play an important role in NAIC's program of investment education: the Investment Discussion List (a.k.a. the I-Club-List) and the NAIC Forum. These discussion forums give users a chance to ask specific questions and provide a network of help and information to members of the NAIC community.

Online Premium Services (OPS) is included the NAIC lifetime membership. Those with NAIC club and individual memberships can subscribe to OPS for an additional charge, and thereby gain access to

- Companies must file a Form 8-K within 15 days of an event that could affect the firm's value.

- Form 13D is filed by any investor who acquires 5% of a company's stock. This alerts management—and the public—that someone may be attempting to buy up shares with perhaps the intent of obtaining control of the company.[4]

financial data on over 10,000 publicly traded companies. A subscription to BITS, the online publication from the NAIC Computer Group, is also included in the OPS subscription.[7]

Please see Chapter 10 for a guide to some of the more informative Web sites.

Summary

It is the obligation of all active investment club members to separate the wheat from the chaff of information sources before doing the same for stocks under consideration by the club.

The library is an all-too-forgotten source of news, knowledge and advice. The local librarian can be your guide to an undiscovered world of wisdom—a living, breathing search engine.

Public corporations (companies whose stock trades on a stock market) are required by law to disclose financial information and provide it to shareholders and to the general public. They do so through annual reports, the 10K report, the corporate quarterly/10Q report and other published information.

Full-service brokerage houses offer clients the full extent of their research services. Discounters also make a certain amount of research available upon request.

Brokerage firms also frequently sponsor free investment seminars.

On the NAIC Web Site, members can use the "Search String" window to access just about every piece of information on the site. Users can also search the I-Club-List for information and comments from other NAIC members.

Chapter Notes

[1] Fritz Williams, *Investing For Life* (Madison Hts., MI: Investment Education Institute, 1997) 90.

[2] Williams 46.

[3] Williams 46.

[4] Williams 46.

[5] Williams 48.

[6] Marsha Bertrand, *Getting Started in Investment Clubs* (New York: John Wiley & Sons, Inc., 2001) 253.

[7] "How the Web Can Work for You," *Better Investing* July 2002: 15-20

Investment Results, Education & NAIC Support

Getting Rich Takes Time[1]

The net worth of most young clubs is typically less than the total of its members' deposits. If your club is showing a profit after the first year or two, odds are that luck, rather than the market, is on your side.

Real wealth takes longer to build. It also takes work. Your membership in the club demonstrates a commitment to investing time as well as money. And that's one of the two most important elements in your eventual success.

And the other one?

It's the base on which to build. That is, the sum of your regular deposits. If you contribute $20 each month, your base will expand by $240 every year.

Figure 9-01 shows how the value of your club account might grow if you earn 8% compounded annually on a ten-dollar monthly investment. In Figure 9-02, you'll see what happens to a twenty-dollar per month investment that earns 15% annually.

Always remember that the market doesn't move in a straight line, and neither will the value of your account. Also remember the Rule of Five.

	FIGURE 9-01: APPRECIATION OF A $10 MONTHLY INVESTMENT AT 8% COMPOUNDED ANNUALLY			
End of Year	Accumulation of $10 Monthly Deposit	8% Annual Earnings (Combined Dividend + Appreciation)	Total Accumulated Earnings	Combined Accumulated Deposits and Earnings
1	120.00	5.14	5.14	125.14
2	240.00	15.15	20.29	260.29
3	360.00	25.96	46.25	406.25
4	480.00	37.74	83.99	563.89
5	600.00	50.15	134.14	734.14
10	1,200.00	130.15	612.83	1,812.83
15	1,800.00	247.56	1,597.79	3,397.79
20	2,400.00	420.07	3,326.61	5,726.61
25	3,000.00	673.53	6,148.41	9,148.41
30	3,600.00	1,044.96	10,575.16	14,176.16

I know. For every five investments, one will outperform expectations, three will about meet them and one will come up short.

Right. There's another element that was somewhast overlooked during the runaway bull market of recent years as being less significant. That could be a mistake in the long run. We're referring to dividends.

As discussed in the DRP section of Chapter 7, dividends are an important part of any investment program, adding to the amount of money available to be invested every month. During extended down periods, they help generate more money with which to make your purchases—hopefully at bargain prices. They add to your compounding rate and add to the club's total to grow.

FIGURE 9-02: APPRECIATION OF A $20 MONTHLY INVESTMENT AT 15% COMPOUNDED ANNUALLY

End of Year	Accumulation of $20 Monthly Deposit	15% Annual Earnings (Combined Dividend + Appreciation)	Total Accumulated Earnings	Combined Accumulated Deposits and Earnings
1	240.00	19.08	19.08	259.08
2	480.00	57.95	77.03	557.03
3	720.00	102.64	179.67	899.67
4	960.00	154.03	333.70	1,293.70
5	1,200.00	213.14	546.84	1,746.84
10	2,400.00	671.42	2,860.36	5,260.36
15	3,600.00	1,593.20	8,727.31	12,327.31
20	4,800.00	3,447.22	21,742.25	26,541.45
25	6,000.00	7,176.30	49,131.15	55,131.15
30	7,200.00	14,676.85	105,435.26	112,635.26

Which is to say, dividends increase both your purchasing and earning powers.

A Philosophy for Building a Fortune[2]

As investors, it is easy to become so involved in trying to find stocks that will appreciate substantially and rapidly that we frequently forget what the basis of real wealth is.

I guess I've forgotten, too. What is it?

The basis of real wealth is the ownership of income-producing properties. The way such properties appreciate determines your ultimate success in investing.

It sounds like Monopoly®.

Good assessment. The person who wins in Monopoly® is the player who gradually acquires the most of the best income-producing properties. Your investment club is like that in many respects. You gradually build the amount of stock you own in good, income-producing properties. If the stock you purchase is in a corporation that is producing good and growing earnings then you, as a shareholder, will enjoy increased income both from growing dividends and from appreciation in the value of that property.

Each month, as you make a deposit in your club and the club purchases a security, you are building your holdings of wealth-producing property. As this fund builds, it begins to produce dividend income for you to purchase more stock—more income-producing property.

When such properties continue to increase income, it is likely that the price of those properties will also increase. As long as they are increasing income, there is probably little reason to sell unless you see signs that they are overvalued, deteriorating in value or that there are other opportunities that seem to be more rewarding (see "Knowing When to Sell" later in this chapter).

But can my monthly contributions really build to a sizeable amount?

Just take another look at Figure 9-02. A six-figure balance from $20 monthly—only $7,200 out of your own pocket over 30 years—seems pretty sizeable to us. Not only that, but in many cases, investment club members use the information acquired to successfully build individual portfolios as well.

Selecting stocks and keeping the emphasis on the point that they represent companies with sound and growing income can greatly reduce the confusion with which you approach the selection process. Growing income, or the demonstrated ability of a corporation to increase its earnings, is the basis of all sound and lasting increases in stock prices.

Judging Investment Results[3]

"If you don't know where you're going, any road will get you there." This bit of cynical wisdom holds a lot of truth, and in your investment club, setting specific money and time goals is the only way to know if you're succeeding. NAIC recommends setting the goal of doubling your money in five years.

I know they do, but why is that?

Because with proper research and diligence, you can reach this goal. Many investment clubs that have subscribed to the NAIC philosophy of stock selection have proven over and over that this goal is realistic.

The five-year interval spans the average time between market peaks. It may take as little as three years or as long as eight years, but five years is the standard used for measuring peak to peak. Because NAIC selection guidelines show you how to judge the value of stocks, you will be able to maximize profits by applying value tests—not only to stocks you're thinking of buying, but also to stocks you already own.

Take the following three steps to answer the question:

> ### HOW WELL IS YOUR CLUB DOING?
>
> 1. Determine your actual rate of return by using the procedure outlined in this chapter.
>
> 2. Evaluate your results against a broadly based market index, such as the S&P 500, which represents the bulk of the total value of NYSE-listed common stocks.
>
> 3. Evaluate your results against those of other clubs of the same age by filling out and returning NAIC's annual performance survey. Forms appear in *Better Investing* during the first quarter of each year. Each club is rated on its lifetime earnings rate as well as their previous year's rate and the club's comparison with the S&P 500 index.

"Success" doesn't demand that you meet or exceed your established standard; setting that goal is only a means of giving yourself a measurement and a focus. As long as your club produces a higher rate of return than you could have achieved through other forms of investing, you're doing a creditable job. And if you're actually earning at the NAIC recommended rate—doubling your money between market peaks—then your club has joined the thousands that have found out that these ideas work.

Calculating Returns

The recommended method for calculating your rate of return (Figure 9-03) is based on the assumption that member contributions have been made every month in unvarying amounts, exclusive of reinvested dividends. Dr. Thomas O. Walton, chairman of the Mathematics Department at Kalamazoo College, under the auspices of local Detroit brokerage firm, developed this calculation. The method recognizes that the true return on an investment is a combination of dividends and market appreciation.

Just follow these steps:

1. Determine the market value of the individual capital account as of the close of the last fiscal year.

2. Determine the total annual individual investment by multiplying the monthly contribution by 12, not including reinvested dividends.

3. Divide the amount in step 1 by the amount in step 2, to the third decimal place.

4. Determine the number of fiscal years over which the annual contribution has been made.

5. Locate the column in Figure 9-3 corresponding to the number of years in step 4.

6. In the column for the number of years, find the number closest to the quotient referred to in step 3.

7. Read down to the row for the percentage figure representing the compound annual rate of increase in the value of the individual capital account.

Examples:

a. Monthly contribution = $10.
Value of individual capital account at end of last fiscal year = $912.12.
Number of fiscal years contribution was made = 6.
Multiply $10 by 12 = $120.
Divide $912.12 by 120 = 7.601.
Locate the number closest to 7.601 in the column for 6 years (the closest number is 7.650).
Read across to 8 percent, which equals the annual rate of increase.

b. Monthly contribution = 20.
Value of individual capital account at end of last fiscal year = $2,017.58.
Number of years contribution was made = 7.
Multiply $20 by 12 = $240.
Divide $2,017.58 by 240 = 8.406.
Locate the number closest to 8.406 in the column for 7 years, which is 8.361.
Read across to 5 percent.

You should note that these answers are approximate and not precise. A ballpark figure is adequate to indicate if your results are in the right direction

Figure 9-03: Compound Annual Rate of Increase

	YEARS									
RATE	1	2	3	4	5	6	7	8	9	10
5%	1.027	2.105	3.237	4.426	5.674	6.985	8.361	9.806	11.323	12.916
6%	1.032	2.126	3.286	4.516	5.819	7.200	8.664	10.216	11.861	13.605
7%	1.038	2.148	3.336	4.607	5.967	7.422	8.979	10.645	12.427	14.335
8%	1.043	2.169	3.385	4.699	6.118	7.650	9.305	11.092	13.022	15.107
9%	1.048	2.191	3.436	4.793	6.273	7.886	9.643	11.559	13.648	15.924
10%	1.053	2.212	3.487	4.889	6.431	8.128	9.994	12.047	14.305	16.788
12%	1.064	2.255	3.590	5.084	6.758	8.633	10.732	13.084	15.718	18.666
14%	1.074	2.299	3.695	5.278	7.098	9.170	11.602	14.231	17.280	20.777
16%	1.085	2.343	3.803	5.497	7.460	9.738	12.333	15.446	19.003	23.128
20%	1.105	2.431	4.023	5.933	8.225	10.975	14.275	18.235	22.987	28.690
24%	1.126	2.522	4.253	6.399	9.060	12.361	16.453	21.527	27.820	35.622
28%	1.146	2.613	4.490	6.894	9.970	13.907	18.947	25.398	33.656	44.225
32%	1.166	2.705	4.736	7.418	10.958	15.631	21.799	29.941	40.688	54.874

and if they are sufficient to bring you close to your goal.

If you meet with initial success, don't allow yourself or fellow club members to become over-confident. As English novelist Samuel Butler said, "Money is like the reputation for ability—more easily made than kept."

And don't be discouraged if you're not ahead of the game from the start. Clubs typically lose money the first year or two, until the effect of reinvested capital gains and dividends begins to have an effect. Remember that you're in the market for the long term.

Commenting in *The Wall Street Journal,* Charles R. Schwab, founder of the major discount brokerage, reminded readers that researchers have convincingly demonstrated that stocks provide superior returns over extended holding periods. Despite this evidence, most people contributing to employer-sponsored defined-contribution plans direct their retirement funds into fixed-rate investments.

Schwab wrote, "I find this disturbing. By taking the low-risk, low-reward path, millions of Americans are limiting their financial future. Take charge of your financial future. No one else can do it for you."

Knowing When to Sell[4]

Famed investing guru Warren Buffet has a theory on the best time to sell: "Never." This may be an extreme position, but amateur investors are more likely to sell too soon than to hold their stocks too long.

But as you say, that's an extreme position; stocks do get sold, and for good reasons. So it still comes down to knowing when to pull the plug and either count your profits or cut your losses.

Consider that with each sell action you must make not one, but two, right decisions. First, you must decide to sell stock A. Then, you must find its replacement. And stock B must offer less downside risk and greater upside potential than its predecessor in order to justify the action.

The decision is not limited to share price. You can't forget commission, either. Brokerage commissions and fees vary widely, depending on the firm you use. Typically, a discount firm will charge less than a full-service firm. Firms operating exclusively online may charge even less. Plus you must add the additional federal and state taxes you and your fellow club members will have to pay on your profits, further eroding your "gross" profit.

Then while we have your attention, you'll want to commit to memory the 14 sell/hold signals in Figures 9-04 and 9-05. There's nothing mystical or masterful about them. It's not done with mirrors; it's done with homework.

FIGURE 9:04: FOR SALE—STOCKS

1. **Because of an adverse management change.** New management is not necessarily good management. It might be difficult for you to assess the ability of brand-new management, but solicit and consider the opinion of investment professionals who may be familiar with the individuals' track records.

2. **Because of declining profit margins.** This is a leading indicator of corporate problems. Keep in mind the Wall Street saying, "There is no such thing as one bad quarter." The company may be in for a year or more of depressed earnings.

3. **Because of a deteriorating corporate financial condition.** If a company has taken on too much debt, it may face serious trouble meeting interest and principal payments in a slowing economy. Keep up to date on changes in the company's capitalization, and check the impact of leverage.

4. **Because competition is affecting profits.** Nobody has a monopoly on a good idea. When others see the potential for a product or service and enter the business, price-cutting, earnings erosion, and even bankruptcy may follow. Don't follow the crowd and chase "in" industries. Think for yourself, and look at the ability of management, not the glamour of the business.

5. **Because of dependence on a single product.** In the 1960s, Brunswick Corporation was viewed as a growth stock. When the automatic bowling pin machine was introduced, bowling lanes throughout the country and abroad made sure to buy it. However, once every bowling facility had the equipment, the growth slowed. This was product growth, contrasted with the growth that stems from good management. Look for companies whose growth estimates are slower than that of a shooting star, but longer lasting.

6. **Because a stock's quality will change as economic circumstances change.** The quality of a stock comprises many factors, including size, financial condition, consumer acceptance, market share, effectiveness of research and depth of management. But if the price of raw materials triples, the stock's attributes are still good, but changes in the economic situation have changed its quality.

7. **Because securities that have proven to be cyclical and that have a recent history of slow growth should be sold when the economy peaks.** Generally speaking, consider buying cyclical stocks during the trough when P/E ratios are relatively high and the market is predicting their earnings recovery. Don't buy when the multiples are relatively low and the stocks seem to be a bargain, as this indicates that earnings are headed for a decline.

8. **Because it's important to maintain balance by company size in your portfolio.** As a general rule, you should keep 25 percent of your holdings in companies with $5 billion or more in sales (large capitalization), and 50 percent in medium-sized companies (mid cap) and 25 percent in small companies with sales less than $500 million (small cap) and rapid growth rates.

FIGURE 9:05: HOLD ON!

1. **Don't sell just because the price hasn't moved.** One of the cardinal requirements for successful investing is patience. Don't concentrate on the price, as a trader would; rather, focus on the fundamentals, as a long-term investor should. If the basics remain attractive, over time you needn't worry about price.

2. **Don't sell because of a paper loss.** You might think it's smart to sell out when a stock declines 10 or 20 percent. But a stock worth keeping can certainly dip that far in a declining market.

3. **Don't sell because of a paper profit.** You might be tempted to sell when a stock doubles, yet many stocks post gains of 2,000 percent and even more over a 10-year span. Think how much you'd have missed if you sold after the first year! Again, concentrate on the study of fundamentals. As long as the stock meets the criteria you have established, hold on to it.

4. **Don't sell on temporary bad news.** One example is Metromedia, which once enjoyed an earnings gain of 40 percent in a quarter when newspapers in two of its major markets were on strike. Advertisers flocked to Metromedia's TV stations, and management pointed out that earnings probably would be less in the same quarter the following year. Sure enough, they were, and the price of the stock fell sharply, even after management's caveat. But as management also predicted, earnings resumed their upward trend, and so did the stock price.

5. **Don't sell just to take action.** This is sometimes appealing if you feel frustrated that something isn't happening quickly enough. Be patient and wait out the market.

6. **Don't sell a stock that has fallen so far that your remaining downside risk is minimal compared to the upside potential.**

If you are unsure about whether to sell, why not hedge your decisions? Sell part of the holding and keep the rest. You'll be diversifying your club's portfolio, which can be especially important if a single issue has become too large a part of it. In a small portfolio (under $40,000), a single issue should not account for more than 20 percent of total value. In a larger portfolio, no single holding should represent more than 10 percent.

Selling may be the most difficult decision you face as investors. Make it a wise one.

Portfolio Management[5]

As your club's portfolio grows with time, portfolio management becomes more important.

What's "portfolio management"?

In a *Better Investing* interview Gary Ball, director of the Puget Sound NAIC Chapter and a national advisory director, offered this definition:

"Portfolio management basically is matching your portfolio to your investment objectives. When you begin building your portfolio, you need to decide what your investment objectives are. Those objectives certainly shouldn't change quickly, but they may change over time."

Not only that, but as Tom O'Hara and Ken Janke advise, many new investors—and a lot of not-so-new ones—overlook the vital importance of managing a security once it is bought. In other words, the stock you bought yesterday is not the one you hold today, because circumstances have surely changed—for better or worse.

Think about it. AT&T today is not your grandfather's stock.

Fifty years ago there were no baby bells, no fiber optics, no competition to speak of. You bought a blue chip such as this one, held onto it and slept well as the dividends rolled in, the price went up and the stock split and split again. And AT&T today? Let's not speak of that, either.

Another common mistake is devoting a disproportionate amount of time to new stock purchases and not enough to watching what you already hold.

In other words, we say "buy and hold" but what we really do is "buy and ignore."

Perfectly put. And Ken Janke, for one, is dismayed "that a new investment is only a small part of the portfolio never seems to occur to some shareholders. If investors spend hours studying a stock in which $5,000 may be invested, why would they ignore a portfolio that could be worth ten times that amount?"

So how much maintenance does our portfolio need?

NAIC's experience suggests that adequate portfolio management entails an annual review of each stock to confirm that it has the potential of doubling in value over the next five years (or whatever your goal for it is) and ensuring that there is good diversification both by industry and by size of company.

But if we're a very young club, how can we diversify?

Quickly, says Gary Ball. "Whether you're investing $100 or $1000 into that first stock," he notes, "you still have only one stock [and] whatever happens is going to happen to your whole portfolio. Get between five and seven stocks in [your] portfolio as quickly as possible."

However, don't carry diversification too far, remind O'Hara and Janke. Know your club's limits and hold only as many stocks as you can watch carefully.

Any tips to doing that?

Your club should organize its portfolio management program so that each holding becomes the responsibility of a single member. You may choose to have portfolio management reviews of individual stocks on an ongoing basis, so that all stocks are covered once a year.

The NAIC Portfolio Management Guide (PMG) not only disciplines club members to examine a stock's price on a regular basis, but also depicts the crucial relationship over time of price to P/E ratio. NAIC's software provides a quick and easy way to prepare this form.

However you structure your reviews of individual holdings,

the club should look at its total portfolio once a year. A chart should be drawn up (see Figure 9-06), showing the current price, estimated five-year low and five-year high for each stock, and with columns showing each stock's size and industry classification.

The purpose of the review is fourfold: (1) to check the diversification of the portfolio by industry, (2) to check the diversification by size, (3) to confirm growth potential and (4) to check valuations.

We have listed the annual revenues of each company (M is millions, B is billions) and then classified it L for very large, M for medium, and S for small.

What's one key to good portfolio management?

Try patience, says NAIC national advisory director Gary Ball. "Sometimes [people] feel that since they've gone to all the trouble to do an NAIC Stock Selection Guide, they ought to buy the stock. But I may do an SSG on five, six, eight—even 10—stocks before finding the best company."

Impatience can lead to other fundamental mistakes. Selling when a stock doesn't move for a while, or because the company has a problem that proves to be transitory, fly in the face of NAIC's basic principles. If you skimmed past Figures 9-04 and 9-05, for example, you may be showing early signs of the kind

of impatience that could prove costly to the club later.

Are you saying don't ever sell?

Not at all. However, getting in and out of the stock market is very dangerous. Studies have shown that individuals who invest in good-quality stocks of companies with a fairly steady increase in sales and earnings levels do better than the investor who moves from one group of stocks to another and in and out of stocks.

One of the reasons that the "switcher" has difficulty succeeding is that when the market changes directions and starts up, the upward movement takes place so quickly that many investors miss the opportunity.

FIGURE 9-06: EXAMPLE OF CLUB PORTFOLIO DISPLAY

	Stock A	Stock B	Stock C	Stock D	Stock E	Cash	Total
Current Shares	350	450	250	150	425		
Current Price	40.625	35.50	67.75	69.75	31.25		
Current Value	14,218	15,975	16,937	10,462	13,281	2,152	73,025
5-Yr. High Price	60	75	83	95	78		
5-Yr. High Value	21,000	33,750	20,750	14,250	33,150	2,152	125,052
5-Yr. Low Price	26	22	56	51	22		
5-Yr. Low Value	9,100	9,900	14,000	7,650	9,350	2,152	52,152
Sales	10.0B	300.0M	27.0B	2.7B	500.0M		
Size	L	S	L	M	M		
Industry	Health	Insurance	Auto	Medical	Telecom		

For instance, John J. Curran, writing in *Fortune,* pointed out that while stocks provided an average annual return of 17.6 percent through the decade of the 1980s, the greater part of the gain took place on just 40 of the 2,528 days the stock market was open during that period. If you were out of the market on those days, your average annual gain would have been only 4 percent.

Wow. Sure makes you want to manage your portfolio to the max.

That's why NAIC offers so many proven tools to do so. Two of these are PERT and the Challenge Tree, which will be given a general treatment here.

PERT is NAIC's Portfolio Evaluation Review Technique. It is a method for systematically following up on stocks and a portfolio in terms of the same fundamentals used in the Stock Selection Guide. It helps to provide you with factual data to assist in a judgment to buy, hold or sell. NAIC computer software programs support PERT and are a great convenience.

The Challenge Tree is a systematic approach to improving the performance of your portfolio. It shows how to compare the merits of one stock against another, using guidelines to avoid some of the hazards of buying and selling stocks. With the Challenge Tree, you will be able to upgrade your portfolio, as any disappointing results become apparent. The Challenge Tree is a proven, consistent method for analyzing holdings and making informed decisions.

NAIC Support

Throughout the pages of this book, you'll find evidence of the unparalleled assistance afforded associates of NAIC. As Kenneth Janke reminds us:

"NAIC's vision is to build a nation of individual investors, and our mission is to provide a program of sound investment information, education and support that helps create successful lifetime investors."[6]

What follows is an overview of the NAIC support program that has produced positive investment results for more than five million people since 1951. Figure 9-07 (a reprise of Figure 3-01) offers thumbnail descriptions of the NAIC investment analysis forms you've learned about in this book, while Figure 9-08 introduces the various resources and services available to you and your club.

FIGURE 9-07: NAIC INVESTMENT ANALYSIS FORMS

FORM	DESCRIPTION
Stock Check List (SCL)	This form helps the new investor review the basic financial information of a stock and develop an opinion of its current value. It serves as an introduction to the Stock Selection Guide.
Stock Selection Guide (SSG)	NAIC's most popular guide to stock analysis. It is designed to help you review the financial history and record of a particular stock and, using your judgment, make an informed investment decision.
Stock Selection Guide and Report (SSG&R)	This four page form includes the SSG and a two page narrative, fill-in the blanks analysis which helps you understand and interpret the SSG.
Stock Comparison Guide (SCG)	This guide helps you make an intelligent comparison of several stocks, such as similar stocks within the same industry. It is designed to aid in the selection of the best potential investment.
Portfolio Management Guide (PMG)	Once you have purchased a stock, follow its sales and earnings record by plotting and graphing stock data over time. The PMG helps you make buy and sell decisions for each stock in your portfolio.
Portfolio Evaluation Review Technique (PERT)	With PERT and PERT Worksheets A and B, investors can follow the monthly progress of all stocks in their portfolio. Track sales, earnings, stock price and more —an essential record of all your securities and portfolio performance.
Challenge Tree Kit (CTK)	This kit and set of forms allows the experienced investor to determine whether or not to continue holding a stock or to replace it with one appearing to have greater potential.
Mutual Fund Forms	1. The Mutual Fund Check List (MFCL) guides the investor through a step-by-step process that examines key elements of a fund that need to be understood prior to considering it for investment.
	2. The Mutual Fund Comparison Guide (MFCG) helps you compare different funds' performance, yields and other factors to determine a potential investment decision.
	3. The Mutual Fund Trend Report (MFTR) is used to log and update criteria for a particular fund purchase, and monitor for changes.

NOTE: NAIC provides software that allows you to complete each of the investment analysis forms above.

FIGURE 9-08: RESOURCES AND SERVICES FOR INVESTMENT CLUBS

NAIC Headquarters Support

Does your club have a question about NAIC tools or programs? Do you need to verify an upcoming Chapter event or order any materials? Call NAIC toll-free at (877) ASK-NAIC (275-6242) or e-mail service@better-investing.org.

NAIC Web Site

A wealth of information awaits on www.better-investing.org. Some of the key areas include: Welcome to NAIC, Frequently Asked Questions, Top 100 Stocks, the NAIC Members-Only area and the Education section. Visit the I-Club listserv to interact with other club members. Check out the free club accounting program and NAIC Software demos.

NAIC Chapter Seminars and Workshops

Local NAIC chapters consist of trained volunteers who teach NAIC principles and tools in seminars, workshops and events for people of all ages and levels of investment experience. Find out about upcoming chapter events by visiting the NAIC Web Site chapter area, read "Chapter Regional Notices" in *Better Investing* magazine, or call the chapter contact.

Over 115 regional chapters across the country hold local NAIC programs. Seminar topics range from youth investing to retirement planning to learning the Stock Selection Guide to computerized investing. Workshops teach the main NAIC tools and may include a guest speaker or other special investment topics.

NAIC Special Events

NAIC Investor's Fairs® are held in more than 75 cities each year, giving attendees access to top corporate executives. The World Investor's Conference is held every two years, providing education to investors worldwide. NAIC's Better Investing Campaign is designed to encourage lifetime investment.

NAIC Conferences

The Better Investing National Convention is NAIC's premier gathering of long-term investors. The three-day event features nationally known speakers, tours, seminars, workshops and one of the largest displays of investment information in the world. Compufest® is an annual assemblage of individuals who are interested in learning to use computers to invest the NAIC way. Investors of all ages and skill levels benefit from software seminars, one-on-one instruction and computer labs.

NAIC Computer Support

NAIC's Computer Group offers members a variety of services, activities, seminars and support to enhance investing skills with computer aids. NAIC Software performs everything from data collection to stock analysis, providing practical, user-friendly applications to make investing tasks easier. NAIC Online offers investors a place to obtain help, share ideas and develop investing skills.

Summary

Real wealth takes time to build. Your commitment to investing time as well as building a monetary base on a regular basis, are the two most important elements in your eventual success.

Dividends are an important part of any investment program. During extended down periods, they help generate money with which to make your purchases. They add to your compounding rate and add to the club's total to grow. Which is to say, dividends increase both your purchasing and earning powers.

The basis of real wealth is the ownership of income-producing properties. The way such properties appreciate determines your ultimate success in investing.

Because NAIC selection guidelines show you how to judge the value of stocks, you will be able to maximize profits by applying value tests—not only to stocks you're thinking of buying, but also to stocks you already own.

Consider that with each sell action you must make not one, but two, right decisions. First, you must decide to sell stock A. Then, you must find its replacement. Stock B must offer less downside risk and greater upside potential than its predecessor in order to justify the action.

Portfolio management is matching your portfolio to your investment objectives. Many new investors overlook the vital importance of managing a security once it is bought.

NAIC's experience suggests that adequate portfolio management entails a quarterly review of each stock to confirm that it has the potential of doubling in value over the next five years (or whatever your goal for it is) and ensuring that there is good diversification both by industry and by size of company.

Your club should organize its portfolio management program so that each holding becomes the responsibility of a single member. You may choose to have portfolio management reviews of individual stocks on an ongoing basis, so that all stocks are covered once a year. The club should look at its total portfolio once a year.

PERT is NAIC's Portfolio Evaluation Review Technique. It is a method for systematically following up on stocks and a portfolio in terms of the same fundamentals used in the Stock Selection Guide.

The Challenge Tree shows how to compare the merits of one stock against another, using guidelines to avoid some of the hazards of buying and selling stocks.

NAIC's mission—to provide a program of sound investment information, education and support—has produced positive investment results for more than five million people since 1951.

Chapter Notes

[1] The NAIC Investment Club Monthly Study Program is used as source material for much of this section.

[2] The NAIC Investment Club Monthly Study Program is used as source material for much of this section.

[3] Much of this section is taken from Thomas E. O'Hara and Kenneth S. Janke, Sr., *Starting and Running a Profitable Investment Club* (New York: Times Books, 1998) 225-228.

[4] Much of this section is taken from O'Hara and Janke 155-158.

[5] This section adapts and updates O'Hara and Janke, 121-153 and features quotations from "In Portfolio Management, Patience is Key," *Better Investing* July 2002: 46-47 and "Don't Ignore Portfolio Management," *Better Investing* August 2001: 12.

[6] NAIC Member User's Guide.

CHAPTER TEN:

Directories of Investment Data, Services & Tools

Educational Web Sites
for Investors

Print Educational Resources

NAIC Publications, Books,
Videos and CDs

NAIC Software

Educational Web Sites for Investors

There are hundreds of sources of online investment information available on the Internet. NAIC has compiled a list of Web sites that you may consider visiting. We hope they will prove valuable in helping you follow NAIC investing principles and become a better investor!

NOTE: The following Web sites are provided only as informational resources for investors. There are a variety of additional sites that investors may use to access investing information. NAIC does not specifically endorse any of the sites listed, or the products, services or promotions they offer.

FIGURE 10-01: INVESTMENT ASSOCIATIONS AND GROUP WEB SITES

www.better-investing.org	National Association of Investors Corporation
www.cfainstitute.org	CFA Institute
www.investoreducation.org	Alliance for Investor Education
www.fraud.org	National Fraud Information Center
www.niri.org	National Investor Relations Institute
www.savers.org	The Savers and Investors League
www.sia.com	Securities Industry Association
www.wfic.org	World Federation of Investors Corporation

FIGURE 10-02: GOVERNMENT WEB SITES

www.pueblo.gsa.gov	Consumer Information Center
www.edgar-online.com	EDGAR—Electronic Data Gathering/Analysis/Retrieval
www.fdic.gov	Federal Deposit Insurance Corporation
www.federalreserve.gov	Federal Reserve Bank Board of Governors
www.irs.gov	Internal Revenue Service
www.sec.gov	Securities and Exchange Commission
www.doc.gov	U.S. Department of Commerce
www.ustreas.gov	U.S. Department of Treasury

FIGURE 10-03: BUSINESS PUBLICATION WEB SITES

www.barrons.com	*Barron's* Magazine
www.better-investing.org	*Better Investing* Magazine
www.economist.com	*The Economist* Magazine
www.financialworld.co.uk/magazine	*Financial World* Magazine
www.forbes.com	*Forbes* Magazine
www.fortune.com	*Fortune* Magazine
www.investors.com	*Investors Business Daily* Newsletter
www.individualinvestor.com	*INVESTools* Newsletters
www.kiplinger.com	*Kiplinger's Personal Finance* Magazine
www.money.cnn.com	CNN and *MONEY* Magazine
www.nytimes.com	*New York Times*
www.smartmoney.com	*Smart Money* Magazine
www.usatoday.com	*USA Today*
www.wsj.com	*Wall Street Journal*
www.worth.com	*Worth* Magazine

FIGURE 10-04: FINANCIAL NEWS AND DATA WEB SITES

www.bloomberg.com	Bloomberg Personal Financial News
www.businesswire.com	Businesswire News
www.money.cnn.com	CNN Financial News
www.dj.com	Dow Jones, Inc.
www.hoovers.com	Hoover's Online Database
www.morningstar.com	Morningstar Mutual Funds
www.better-investing.org	National Association of Investors Corporation Online Premium Services, stock data
www.prnewswire.com	PR Newswire
www.reuters.com	Reuters Financial News
www.standardandpoors.com	Standard & Poor's
www.bigcharts.com	Stock prices, financial information
www.valueline.com	Value Line Investment Report

FIGURE 10-05: STOCK EXCHANGE WEB SITES

www.amex.com	American Stock Exchange
www.bostonstock.com	Boston Stock Exchange
www.chicagostockex.com	Chicago Stock Exchange
www.cboe.com	Chicago Board Options Exchange
www.nasdaq.com	The NASDAQ Stock Market, Inc.
www.nyse.com	New York Stock Exchange
www.phlx.com	Philadelphia Stock Exchange
www.pacificex.com	Pacific Stock Exchange

FIGURE 10-06: YOUTH AND INVESTING WEB SITES

www.jumpstartcoalition.org	Jump Start Coalition (youth financial literacy)
www.japersonalfinance.org	Junior Achievement
www.better-investing.org	NAIC Web Site youth area
www.italladdsup.org	National Council on Economic Education
www.ntrbonline.org	National Endowment for Financial Education
www.smg2000.com	The Stock Market Game
www.youngbiz.com	Young Biz (business)
www.economicsamerica.org	Young Economic Education
www.younginvestor.com	A mutual fund youth education site

FIGURE 10-07: OTHER INVESTOR WEB SITES

www.dripinvestor.com	Charles Carlson, author of the Drip Investor Newsletter maintains this site.
www.money.cnn.com/pf	CNN/Money Magazine's Personal Finance Center
www.fool.com	The Motley Fool
www.naupa.org	National Association of Unclaimed Property Administrators (help in regaining lost stock certificates, uncollected dividends or other lost investment instruments)
finance.yahoo.com	Yahoo finance site

Print Educational Resources

FIGURE 10-08: INVESTMENT RESEARCH SERVICES

Analyst Watch

A report of earnings estimates published by Zacks Investment Research.

Donoghue'$ Money Letter

This guide to stock funds, bond funds and money market funds includes mutual fund asset allocation models for conservative, active or venturesome portfolios.

Earnings Guide

Published by Standard & Poor's, with earnings forecasts of stocks for the next quarter and each of the next two years.

Emerging and Special Situations

Published by Standard & Poor's, with a New Issues supplement. Advice for those interested in small capital stocks, including a recommended list.

Growth Stock Outlook

Designed for those "who recognize the risk and rewards of investing in vigorously growing companies."

Handbook for No-Load Fund Investors

Published by the No-Load Fund Investor Advisory Service. A directory of no-load stock and bond funds, along with ten-year performance data on the funds and a section on how to pick and monitor funds.

Handbook of Common Stocks

Published by Moody's, this handbook provides overviews of stocks with high investor interest.

Handbook of Dividend Achievers

Published by Moody's. Lists companies that have increased their annual dividend payout for ten consecutive years or more.

Handbook Guide to Financial Newsletters

Issued by the New York Institute of Finance, this reference rates investment newsletters by clarity of advice, completeness, relative risk and volatility.

Industry Reports

Published by Standard & Poor's and containing information on business sectors from aerospace to utilities.

Industry Review

Published by Moody's, this loose-leaf service provides comparative key financial and operating data on corporations covering 145 industry groups.

Industry Surveys

Economic and business information from Standard & Poor's on industry groups, including key financial data on individual companies.

FIGURE 10-08: INVESTMENT RESEARCH SERVICES

Moody's Dividend Record Service

The service covers common and preferred dividend-paying stocks, mutual funds, foreign securities and nonpaying issues.

Morningstar Mutual Fund Source Book

Two-volume coverage of equity and fixed-income funds.

Morningstar Mutual Funds

Published in two sections. The first section classifies load and no-load equity and fixed income funds by risk, objective, total return, dividends and net assets. Portfolio manager changes are included. The second section presents detailed information of selected funds.

Mutual Fund ProFiles

Published by Standard & Poor's and Lipper Analytical Services. Covers funds comprising general and specialized equity funds, balanced funds and long-term taxable fixed income mutual funds. Description includes investment policy, performance evaluation, portfolio composition and five-year historical data.

Nelson's Earnings Outlook

A compilation of estimated earnings per share based on figures supplied by security analysts who follow particular stocks and industries.

No-Load Fund Investor

Provides comprehensive coverage of virtually all no-load funds available to the public, plus direct marketed low-loads and closed-ends. Offers performance data for seven periods ranging from the latest month to five years. Includes cash positions and betas.

The Outlook

Published by Standard & Poor's. Covers the status of the stock market, lists stock to buy and stocks to avoid, and features a stock from S&P's Master List of Recommended Stocks for Superior Long-Term Total Return.

S&P Earnings Guide

A compilation of estimated earnings per share based on figures supplied by security analysts who follow particular stocks and industries.

S&P Industry Report Service

Provides a comprehensive look at business sectors from aerospace to utilities, offering fundamental and investment forecasts by industry and buy and sell recommendations on individual stocks within the groupings. Lists companies by industry.

FIGURE 10-08: INVESTMENT RESEARCH SERVICES

S&P Stock Guide
A pocket-sized alphabetical guide to common and preferred stocks, both listed and over-the-counter. A special section contains data on selected leading mutual funds.

S&P Stock Report Services
Popularly known as S&P sheets, the service offers salient statistics on selected companies listed on the New York, American and regional stock exchanges, as well as over-the-counter issues.

Stock Market Encyclopedia
Published by Standard & Poor's. Includes data on industrial, utility, transportation and financial firms. A full-page report is included for every stock in the S&P 500.

Value Line Investment Survey
Published by Value Line Publishing, Inc. Follows stocks and industries in three sections: Summary and Index, Selection and Opinion, and Ratios and Reports.

Value Line Mutual Fund Survey
Offers extensive information on established funds and presents data on selected newer and smaller funds.

Wall Street Digest
Digest of investment advice from leading financial advisors.

FIGURE 10-09: INDEXES AND DIRECTORIES

America's Corporate Families and International Affiliates
Published by Dun & Bradstreet, linking U.S. and foreign parents with the domestic and international affiliates.

Brands and Their Companies
Published by Gale Research Inc., providing access to consumer brands, manufacturers and importers.

Bull & Bear's Directory of Investment Advisory Newsletters
Published by Bull & Bear Financial Newspaper, Inc. Lists newsletters within each category, including international investments, mutual funds, new issues and stocks.

Business and Investment Almanac
Published by Business One Irwin. A review of the year, including stock market averages, prices/earnings ratios, foreign stock markets, mutual fund performance and more. Includes an explanation of investment and financial terms.

Business Periodicals Index
Published by H.W. Wilson Company. An index to the contents of several hundred periodicals.

Corporate Directory of U.S. Public Companies
Published by Walker's Western Research. Detailed data on selected firms.

FIGURE 10-09: INDEXES AND DIRECTORIES

Corporation Records
Published by Standard & Poor's. Financial information on selected companies.

Directory of Companies Offering Dividend Reinvestment Plans
Published by Evergreen Enterprises. Dividend reinvestment plans listed for selected corporations and closed-end investment companies.

Directory of Dividend Reinvestment Plans
Published by Dow Theory Forecasts Inc. Includes business profiles, plan specifics, company performance ratings and address and telephone information.

Dun & Bradstreet Reference Book of American Business
Contains information on millions of U.S. companies.

Dun's Business Rankings
Published by Dun & Bradstreet. Ranks top firms by sales and employees.

Encyclopedia of Associations
Published by Gale Research, Inc.

Encyclopedia of Business Information Sources
Published by Gale Research, Inc. A guide to subjects of interest to business people.

Gale Directory of Databases
Published by Gale Research, Inc. Profiles databases to reveal which cover subjects of interest, where and how to access them and what you'll find when you do.

Investment Statistics Locator
Published by Oryx Press. Detailed subject index to the most-used sources of financial and investment data.

Million Dollar Directory: America's Leading Public and Private Companies
Published by Dun & Bradstreet, offers information on selected top businesses.

Moody's Complete Corporate Index
Comprehensive index to corporations included in Moody's Manuals.

Moody's Manuals
Comprehensive statistical and analytical data covering listed and unlisted industrials, public utilities, transportation companies, banks and finance companies, and international businesses.

New York Times Index
Business listings indexed by industry, individual company, and person.

Predicates F and S Index—United States
Selectively indexes leading business publications for company activities, industry news and product information.

Principal International Businesses
Published by Dun & Bradstreet, offering up-to-date information on leading enterprises around the world.

Reader's Guide to Periodical Literature
Published by H.W. Wilson Company. A cumulative author/subject index to periodicals of general interest.

FIGURE 10-09: INDEXES AND DIRECTORIES

Reference Book on Corporate Managements
Published by Dun & Bradstreet, lists biographies of top corporate executives.

Register of Corporations, Directors and Executives
Published by Standard & Poor's.

Statistical Abstract of the U.S.
Published by the Bureau of the Census. Contains U.S. industrial, economic, political and social statistics.

Stock Market Encyclopedia
Published by Standard & Poor's. Includes data on industrial, utility, transportation and financial firms. A full-page report is included for every stock in the S&P 500.

Wall Street Journal Index
Published by Dow Jones.

Wiesenberger Investment Companies Service
Includes general information about funds as an investment medium, as well as descriptions of and data on investment companies.

FIGURE 10-10: NEWSPAPERS AND MAGAZINES

Barron's
Published by Dow Jones & company. Contains articles on industries and companies, commentary on stock market activity, information on new issues, a summary of research reports, and a comprehensive statistical section including both current and year-ago earnings information.

Better Investing
Monthly magazine of NAIC containing information designed especially for the self-reliant investor. Features include a stock to study, an undervalued stock, selected portfolios, and regular columnists who provide a variety of investment information and ideas.

Business Week
Covers the general business scene, with departments focusing on the economy, government, finance, science and technology, and personal business, among other topics.

FW (formerly Financial World)
Departments include market watch, company watch, economic currents, market comments and special situations.

Forbes
Sections include international, companies/industries, money and investing, law and issues, marketing, computers, science and technology, and personal affairs. Also featured are regular columnists.

FIGURE 10-10: NEWSPAPERS AND MAGAZINES

Fortune

Coverage includes the economy, innovation, technology, and money and markets. Departments include personal investing.

Investor's Business Daily

Gives complete market quotes and a variety of statistical information along with news stories.

Kiplinger's Personal Finance

Topics include spending, taxes, estate planning, investing basics, insurance and personal finances.

MONEY

Areas of concern include home ownership, jobs, taxes, insurance and investing.

The New York Times

The business section, daily and Sunday, is the nation's most comprehensive.

Smart Money

From Hearst Corporation and Dow Jones, covering investing, insurance, taxes, travel and business books.

USA Today

A national daily with extensive quotations and business news.

The Wall Street Journal

Published by Dow Jones & Company. Issued Monday through Friday in regional editions, reporting news developments in terms of their significance to business people and investors.

Wall Street Transcript

Published by Wall Street Transcript Corporation. Provides reprints of investment research reports, roundtable discussions and industry features.

FIGURE 10-11: NEWSLETTERS

Direct Purchase/Dividend-Reinvestment News

Published by David Blackburn. Lists companies. Furnishes data on discounts, minimum and maximum share purchases and any sales charges.

DRIP Investor

News and guidance on investing through dividend reinvestment plans.

Growth Stock Outlook

Published by Charles Allmon. Designed for those "who recognize the risks and rewards of investing in vigorously growing companies."

No-Load Fund Investor

Provides comprehensive coverage of no-load and direct-marketed no-loads.

NAIC Publications, Books, Videos & CDs

NAIC offers club members and individuals a wide variety of educational products and tools to help build investing knowledge and experience. These tools guide and teach the user to become an informed and successful investor. NAIC stock study and mutual fund tools are designed for easy understanding and help analyze and compare potential investments, record their progress, manage portfolios and achieve many other objectives that lead to investment success.

FIGURE 10-12: NAIC PUBLICATIONS

Better Investing Magazine	Each monthly issue keeps you up to date on all the latest investment information and NAIC club news, helping you make better-informed investment decisions.
Better Investing BITS	The NAIC computer group online newsletter focuses on the "how to" in using computer aids to invest the NAIC way.
Young Money Matters	A newsletter for young investors that features real-life stories of their experiences, educational exercises and games to teach youth about money concepts, saving and investing.
Investment Analysis and Portfolio Management Forms	NAIC publishes over one dozen forms and guides designed to study, select and track stocks and mutual funds. Sample assortments are also available.

FIGURE 10-13: NAIC BOOKS

Better Investing Book Series	A unique book series designed to enhance educational opportunities for investors. These publications provide an educational self-learning pathway for individuals and club members to become successful long-term investors. This series offers titles for beginner, intermediate and experienced investors. Contact NAIC for pricing and availability.
	1) **NAIC Official Guide—Introduction to Successful Investing Handbook.** This book offers an excellent introduction to investing the NAIC way for individuals and investment clubs. Outlines an easy-to-understand approach to starting a long-term investment program, understanding how to make choices about personal finance and making informed investment decisions.

FIGURE 10-13: NAIC BOOKS

Better Investing Book Series (continued)

1) *NAIC Official Guide—Introduction to Successful Investing Handbook* **(continued).** Throughout the book, it includes information on NAIC's history, philosophy, stock and mutual fund programs.

2) *NAIC Stock Selection Handbook.* A step-by-step self-learning course helping you build a sound understanding of the NAIC Stock Selection Guide. The most comprehensive publication for learning and using NAIC's premier stock analysis form to help you successfully select stocks.

3) *NAIC Mutual Fund Handbook.* This publication provides the investor with a solid background on how to understand and successfully approach mutual fund investing. It also provides instruction on how to learn and use NAIC's mutual fund tools. A powerful learning tool on its own or with the Mutual Fund Interactive Tutorial on CD-ROM.

4) *NAIC Investing for Life—Youth Handbook.* A complete personal finance and investing course for young investor. This self-study course designed for youth and teenagers lays a solid foundation of general knowledge about setting personal and financial goals, saving and investing. It also includes a section on learning the NAIC Stock Selection Guide—great tutorial and self-learning experience for any beginner investor.

5) *NAIC Computerized Investing & the Internet Handbook.* This book offers an introduction to the world of investing with your computer. It provides a solid understanding of how to gain benefits from computerized investing and how to use financial resources on the Internet to help you become a more successful investor.

6) *NAIC Using Portfolio Management Wisdom Handbook.* A publication offering instruction on the use and benefits of NAIC's portfolio management form and techniques. Written in a format for intermediate or experienced investors to advance their knowledge and education.

FIGURE 10-13: NAIC BOOKS

***Better Investing* Book Series (continued)**

7) NAIC Investment Club Operations Handbook. Provides comprehensive information about starting an investment club. It offers detailed steps to organizing your club and ensuring success. Computer CD-ROM bonus included. Also available is a supplemental workbook with lessons and exercises for club members to follow in the first two years of the club experience. These are must-have resources for all new clubs.

8) NAIC Investment Club Accounting Handbook. Includes complete and updated instructions to establish and follow an accurate and efficient method of investment club record keeping. Provides instructions on the use of three club accounting methods: manual paper club accounting forms, Investment Club Accounting Software and online Club Accounting. An excellent resource for club treasurers.

From Little Acorns Grow: Main Street Millionaires

The inspiring story of Thomas E. O'Hara, founder and past president of NAIC.

Investing in Your Future
(South-Western Educational Publishing)

A high school/junior college text workbook teaches students all they need to know about saving and investing. An Instructor's Edition is also available.

FIGURE 10-14: NAIC VIDEOS AND CD-ROMS

Basics to Investing

A beginner's video providing an introduction to NAIC's long-term investing principles as well as its proven investing methods and techniques.

***Better Investing* School Seminars (CD-ROM)**

A 10-part series of educational seminars providing a self-learning computerized tutorial. Designed especially for beginner investors who want to learn about investing using NAIC tools.

Figure 10-14: NAIC Videos and CD-ROMs

Better Investing School Seminars (CD-ROM) (continued)

The seminars include visual and audio commentary including these topics: How to Become a Successful Investor; Using NAIC Tools, Resources and Programs, Stock Check List, Stock Selection Guide & Stock Comparison Guide; Starting an Investment Club; When to Sell; Mutual Fund Investing; What to Ask a Company; and additional resources. Great for introducing beginners or a new investment club to NAIC principles of investing. Seminars use PowerPoint software (software not included).

BITV—Video Series

A 13-part educational video series that includes some of the best features NAIC's *Better Investing* magazine can offer. Hosted by David Chilton, author of *The Wealthy Barber,* this series is a lively and entertaining exploration of the investment philosophies that NAIC is founded upon. Each episode contains 30 minutes or more of investor information, education and insights based on NAIC's principles of long-term investing. This is a timeless educational offering that will provide benefits for beginner to experienced investors. Program topics include: Common Stock Market Mistakes; Earning to Learn—Saving for College; Mutual Funds; Stocks to Study; Questions from Main Street; Wall Street Analysis and Comments; and more. For more information, visit this NAIC Web Site: www.better-investing.tv.

How to Run an Effective Investment Club Meeting Video

An overview of programs and services available from NAIC along with step-by-step guidelines for running a successful investment club meeting. Included in the Investment Club Welcome Packet.

Selecting Equity Mutual Funds Video and CD-ROM Tutorial

Covers NAIC's three analysis tools: Mutual Fund Check List, Comparison Guide and Trend Report, including information provided in the *Mutual Fund Handbook.*

Stock Selection Guide Video

An easy way to teach others or improve your own understanding of the SSG and make better-informed investment decisions.

NAIC Software

NAIC software is dedicated to providing practical, "people-friendly" applications that enhance learning and ease the investing tasks of individuals and investment clubs. NAIC has established alliances with investment software development professionals to bring you products that will perform everything from data collection and stock analysis to record keeping and portfolio management.

Special arrangements have been made to ensure you receive the technical support you need, and a listing of vendor contacts and telephone numbers is included with each software package.

Unlike many other investment packages, NAIC software is designed around the concept that you are capable of making profitable, long-term investment decisions. Each analysis program is richly interactive, allowing multiple opportunities to exercise your judgment and build your investing knowledge.

FIGURE 10-15: NAIC SOFTWARE

NAIC Classic	Designed especially for beginners, *NAIC Classic* provides a carefully structured learning experience. The Stock Wiz character helps investors to become comfortable with completing stock studies in a logical and consistent manner. NAIC *Classic* is a personal tutor that helps the user learn and understand NAIC investing techniques and principles more quickly and thoroughly.
NAIC Club Accounting Software	Friendly and easy-to-use, *NAIC Club Accounting Software* prepares anyone to become their club's treasurer. Designed to work hand-in-hand with the *NAIC Investment Club Accounting Handbook,* it helps new clubs begin with computerized accounting and allows established clubs to easily transfer their existing books, following NAIC recommendations. Includes one year of Customer Support with free online software updates to stay in compliance with U.S. tax laws.
NAIC Investor's Toolkit	Offers everything required to select and evaluate winning stocks, using NAIC's copyrighted forms. Several levels of teaching and assistance are incorporated into the program. *Investor's Toolkit ProMaker* may be purchased at a later date to upgrade *Toolkit.*
NAIC Portfolio Record Keeper	Designed by professional money managers, this wide-ranging yet easy-to-use program provides detailed accounting for investment transactions and portfolio management. Includes tracking features for a variety of security types, powerful graphing tools and Internet connections to popular investment Web sites.

FIGURE 10-15: NAIC SOFTWARE

STB Prospector II

Prospector II is a screening program that helps identify companies that have specific characteristics, and is a must for anyone using stock datafiles. Select from any or all of 120 items to use as screening parameters. *Prospector II* also calculates industry averages. An optional Wizard gets results easily and quickly for the beginner. A free demo program is available on the NAIC Web Site.

STB Stock Analyst PLUS!

A versatile, easy-to-use analysis program to help select, monitor and manage stocks using time-tested NAIC methods. Suitable for both less experienced and advanced users, many professionals use it to manage their clients' portfolios. *Stock Analyst PLUS!* is the most comprehensive software of its type in the marketplace.

Additional software notes:
1. Please visit NAIC's Web Site for the most current information on NAIC software.
2. Free NAIC software demos are available on the Web Site.
3. Owners of previous versions of NAIC software should contact NAIC for availability of software upgrades.
4. NAIC prices and product availability are subject to changae.
5. NAIC software cannot be returned after 30 days from purchase date. Limitations apply to returns within 30 days.

Whether your club is composed of first-time investors, experienced investors or a combination, it's easy to begin and progress at your own pace using NAIC tools and resources. Chart your course using this four-step guide path.

FIGURE 10-16: USING NAIC TOOLS AND RESOURCES

First Step

Read and review NAIC books, videos, publications and educational materials. These tools provide a solid foundation for understanding proven methods of long-term investing.

Second Step

Visit the NAIC Web Site and discover the wealth of information available to you. Build your investing knowledge, review the investing experience of others and share ideas in an online community.

Third Step

Attend NAIC regional chapter seminars, workshops and events to learn successful long-term investing techniques in a hands-on environment and interact with other investors in your community. Trained volunteers will teach you how to use NAIC tools.

Fourth Step

Continue to use NAIC tools, guides, software and local support to help build confidence in selecting growth stocks and mutual funds. Get involved in the NAIC community of investors both in your area and online.

NOTES

Index

INDEX

Pass on the Gift of Lifetime Investing!

Send a Free NAIC Investor's Kit to a Family Member or Friend

Help a family member, friend, neighbor or co-worker become a successful long-term investor... the NAIC Way! Send us their name and we will mail them a free NAIC Investor's Kit. This kit will include information introducing them to NAIC long-term investment methods, programs and tools. The kit will also explain the benefits of lifetime investing including guidelines for starting an investment program on your own or with an investment club.

To send a free NAIC Investor's Kit to someone you know—complete the information below and mail, fax or e-mail the information to NAIC, or contact NAIC by calling toll free: 1-877-275-6242.

Help others you know become successful long-term investors... *the NAIC way!*

Mail to:
NAIC
P.O. Box 220
Royal Oak, MI 48068

___ **YES, please send an NAIC Investor's Kit
to the following person:**

Name _____

Address_____

City_____**State**_____**Zip**_____

e-mail _____

FAX: 248-583-4880
e-mail: service@better-investing.org
NAIC Web Site: www.better-investing.org

Investment Education Since 1951

The National Association of Investors Corporation (NAIC) is a non-profit organization of individual investors and investment clubs, based in Madison Heights, Michigan. Founded in 1951, NAIC's mission is to increase the number of individual investors though investing in common stocks and equity mutual funds, and to provide a program of investment education and information to help its members become successful, long-term investors. NAIC helps investors start a lifetime investment program by following NAIC's Four Investment Principles:

1) *Invest a set sum regularly over your lifetime*
2) *Reinvest earnings and dividends*
3) *Buy growth stocks and mutual funds that concentrate on growth companies*
4) *Diversify your investments*

NAIC members who follow these investment principles have become successful investors over time.

To learn how to start a lifetime investment program using NAIC's proven methods, contact NAIC today.

National Association of Investors Corporation
711 West 13 Mile Road
Madison Heights, MI 48071
1-877-ASK-NAIC (275-6242)
www.better-investing.org

About the Author

Jon Katz has written, produced, directed or performed a wide variety of audio-visual and print projects including radio and television commercials, corporate videos/CDs, full-length books, business meetings, interactive distance learning broadcasts, Web sites, magazine and newsletter articles, executive speeches and many other wide-ranging assignments.

He was a creative vice-president of a Detroit-area advertising agency before founding Katz Creative, Inc. in 1995, and has written for talents such as Tim Allen, Joe Namath, Cliff Robertson and Soupy Sales. Katz has won dozens of national and international awards, including honors from the New York International Film and TV Festival, the International Television Association and the U.S. Industrial Film Festival. In 1974, one of the first radio commercials he wrote and produced won the Best Radio Spot Award from the National Retail Advertising Conference. It featured an impression of W.C. Fields, which Katz performed himself. He has also won two Detroit Emmy Awards and has been recognized as an honorary "Everyday Hero" by the American Red Cross for writing and producing one of their annual awards shows.

An accomplished stage actor and director, Katz has applied his unique and entertaining combination of skills to a variety of writing projects, including theatre and motion picture reviews. He continues to contribute to a diverse group of national periodicals, from the television industry's *Shoot* trade magazine to the *Paw Street Journal,* a newsletter for veterinarians.

In addition to this work; *NAIC Investment Club Operations Handbook,* Jon Katz has authored *NAIC Mutual Fund Handbook* (2000 edition) as well as the *NAIC Investor Advisory Service* video. And these are just three of his over-25,000 credits, spanning a career that began as a college disc jockey in 1968. Other books that Katz has contributed to include *Passing the Bucks: Protecting Your Wealth from One Generation to the Next* (written by Norman Pappas, published by BookCrafters), *Greater Detroit: The First City of the Midwest* (Heritage Media Corporation) and *The Legend of Guardian Industries* (written by Jeffrey L. Rodengen, published by Write Stuff Enterprises).

A graduate of Boston University's College of Communication (B.S.) and Bowling Green State University (M.A.), Katz is a member of the Media Communicators Association—International, Michigan Media Professionals, the Screen Actors Guild and the American Federation of Television and Radio Artists. He lives with his wife and three children in Rochester, Michigan.